What Does
the Bible
Say About... **?**

Old Age

"What Does the Bible Say About...?" Series
Ronald D. Witherup, P.S.S.
Series Editor

What Does
the Bible
Say About... **?**

Old Age

Ronald D. Witherup, P.S.S.

New City Press
Hyde Park, New York

Published by New City Press
202 Comforter Blvd.,
Hyde Park, NY 12538
www.newcitypress.com

Cover design and layout by Miguel Tejerina

Some information in this book was originally published in much briefer form in "What the Bible Says About Growing Old," St. Anthony Messenger 115:2 (2007): 34-38. The author is grateful to Franciscan Media (website: StAnthonyMessenger.org) for permission to reuse this material in an expanded format.

What does the Bible say about Old Age
ISBN: paperback: 978-1-56548-695-9
ISBN: e-book: 978-1-56548-696-6
ISBN: series: 978-1-56548-697-3

Library of Congress Control Number: 2019942349

Printed in the United States of America

Contents

Series Preface

The Bible remains the world's number one best-seller of all time. Millions of copies in more than two thousand languages and dialects are sold every year, yet how many are opened and read on a regular basis? Despite the impression the Bible's popularity might give, its riches are not easy to mine. Its message is not self-evident and is sometimes hard to relate to our daily lives.

This series addresses the need for a reliable guide to reading the Bible profitably. Each volume is designed to unlock the Bible's mysteries for the interested reader who asks, "What does the Bible say about...?" Each book addresses a timely theme in contemporary culture, based upon questions people are asking today, and explaining how the Bible can speak to these questions as reflected in both Old and New Testaments.

Ideal for individual or group study, each volume consists of short, concise chapters on a biblical theme in non-technical language, and in a style accessible to all. The expert authors have been chosen for their knowledge of the Bible. While taking into account current scholarship, they know how to explain the Bible's teaching in simple language. They are also able to relate the biblical message to the challenges of today's Church and society while avoiding a simplistic use of the biblical text for trying to "prove" a point or defend a position, which is called "prooftexting"—an improper use of the Bible. The focus in these books is on a religious perspective, explaining what the Bible says, or does not say, about each theme. Short discussion questions invite sharing and reflection.

So, take up your Bible with confidence, and with your guide explore "what the Bible says about OLD AGE."

Introduction

Both of my parents lived to what we like to call "a ripe old age." My father survived some months into his ninety-third year and was mentally alert and as sharp as ever almost until the day he died. In contrast, my mother, who died at age ninety-seven nearly fourteen years after my father's death, had a difficult decline. The last six years of her life were particularly hard to watch. She suffered from Alzheimer's disease—a frequent diagnosis these days. My siblings and I basically watched her lose not only her vitality but also her personality, her very identity. She did not, in the end, know who we were. But we knew who she was—the matriarch of the family.

This scenario is not unique. Since people live longer than ever in modern times, one notices differences in how people age. Some seem to enter old age gracefully. Like a delicious fruit that matures on a tree and develops a deeper, more intense flavor, so some people seem to flourish with age. They do not merely wither away. They develop more complexity, and, as we traditionally say, greater "wisdom." There are, of course, others. We rail against "dirty old men" and "selfish old biddies." We can become impatient as the elderly slow down, take up more room on sidewalks and in supermarket aisles, drive cars in annoying ways, repeat the same stories over and over again, are very fussy and hard to please, and take up more of our time and energy for their care. On the other hand, we smile when we see old, wrinkled faces in nursing homes come alive with smiles and twinkling eyes in the presence of a baby, a kitten, or a puppy. Or perhaps when their face breaks into a smile as they recognize a loved one coming to visit them. One cannot consider old age without reflecting, to some degree, on the stages of life by which we arrive there.

Whatever we may think of it, old age is more and more a reality in modern life. By virtue of better nurture and health care in many parts of the world, people are living longer. Becoming a centenarian used to be a great milestone. You received a letter from the president, or perhaps an apostolic blessing from the pope. Nowadays centenarians are practically a dime a dozen. The oldest person in recorded recent history died at 116. And she was reputedly quite alert till the end.

Do you plan to grow old? Would you *like* to grow old? Do you think you have a choice? My Uncle John used to say, with a twinkle in his eye, "It sure beats the alternative!"

Many people fear old age. It is coupled with our natural fear of death, no doubt. But the reality of old age has been around, literally, for ages. The purpose of this little book is to put a biblical perspective on old age. What wisdom can we glean from the Bible that might help us better understand the mystery of growing old? It is not intended to be a comprehensive synthesis of biblical teaching. Rather, our approach will be to pick and choose sample texts from the Old Testament and the New Testament that can help illustrate the way the biblical authors viewed the challenges of old age. These passages can still provide us guidance. There is surprising wisdom in these ancient texts that can shed light on our own modern reflections. Along the way, we will add insights from later texts that relate to the themes we touch upon. While it will be most helpful to keep a copy of your Bible handy, many of the biblical texts we will examine will be quoted in full. So, get ready to engage old age with the wisdom of the ages.

Chapter One

Recycled Teenagers

About fifteen years ago I went to my elderly parents' home for a holiday. We decided to go for a customary walk around town and proceeded to put on jackets and walking shoes. My father showed up sporting a new hat from his extensive collection. He had received most of these as gifts. What else do you give an old man who needs fewer and fewer material goods?

In any case, this cap proudly announced: "I'm not old. I'm a recycled teenager!" I had never seen the expression before. He explained that one of the grandchildren had found it in some tourist shop and given it to him as a gift. What was so surprising was that he was inordinately proud of it. All of us in the family knew that he complained considerably about growing old. He always felt cold; his food did not taste the same; he had trouble going up and down steps; he had to frequent bathrooms often, most vexingly in the middle of the night; and he had multiple small aches and pains. "Old age is hell," he would say. Others would add, "Old age is not for the weak!"

Yet here he was advertising that he was *not* old (despite appearances)—he was a recycled version of himself as an adolescent. He liked the idea of being a "recycled teenager."

In fact, despite his age and increasing health problems, my father remained remarkably spry, especially mentally. If his short-term memory was a bit rusty, his long-term memory was often in high gear. He could regale us with tales of his exploits as a young man, some of which were a little risqué for my mother. He could also still recite by heart a long poem that he had had to memorize in grade school.

We have all known people who seem to remain "young at heart" despite their chronological age. I never cease to admire them. Their response to being "time-challenged"—as I overheard one old-timer call it—appears to defy the rules of aging. Even if they no longer retain the same energy or swift reflexes, nevertheless they hold up well because their attitude is positive and they do not allow age to *define* them.

But what about the Bible, as regards old age? One person, upon hearing that I intended to write this book, simply responded: "Oh, it will be a mighty short book! All you have to say is that gray hair and wisdom are the marks of old age." This opinion—which is quite prevalent, I think—is partially correct, but not totally. The Bible, in fact, has a broader teaching than that. It can help us reflect on old age in a deeper way than we might imagine.

Old Age in Biblical Times

One of the most evident truths of the biblical perspective on old age was that it was desirable. Old age was considered a blessing from God, not a scourge. One finds this point of view already in the first book of the Bible, Genesis. The reader will likely remember the fantastic ages of the some of the people in this book, which is devoted to the patriarchs and matriarchs of Israel from time immemorial. Just look at this list of ages.

Adam, the first human being, whose name means "earth being" because he was formed from the dust (Hebrew 'adam) of the earth (Genesis 2:7), is said to have lived 930 years (5:5)! In fact, Genesis says he fathered a son, Seth, at the age of 130 (5:3) and then went on to live another 800 years. (That is some fortitude!) This same Seth is then said to have lived to the age of 912 and to have fathered a son when he was only 105 (5:7-8). Like father, like son, perhaps.

But these only begin the list of fantastic ages in Genesis chapter 5. It continues, with the following key figures:

Enosh = 905

Kenan = 910

Mahalalel = 895

Jared = 962

Enoch = 365 (the youngster of the bunch)

Lamech, the father of Noah = 777 (the lucky number!)

The "granddaddy" of them all, of course, was Methuselah. He is the source of the adage, "as old as Methuselah," that we still use to speak of people in greatly advanced age. Here is what the biblical text says:

When Methuselah had lived one hundred eighty-seven years, he became the father of Lamech. Methuselah lived after the birth of Lamech seven hundred eighty-two years, and had other sons and daughters. Thus all the days of Methuselah were nine hundred sixty-nine years; and he died. (Genesis 5:25-27)

No wonder he is the stellar example of long life! I love the brevity of the text after recounting his incredible age: "and he died"! He must have been tired. He lived 969 years, dying in the year of the great flood, for which God tells Noah to build his ark (Genesis 6:14-22). Noah himself is said to have lived to the age of 950, having fathered his sons Shem, Ham, and Japheth when he was a mere 500 years old (5:32). And these are not the only ones mentioned in Genesis. The unbelievable list of extreme ages continues in Genesis 11:10-26 with Arpachshad (438 years), Shelah (433 years), Eber (464 years), Peleg (239 years), Reu (239 years), Seroug (230 years), Nahor (148 years), and Terah, the father of Abraham (205 years).

Notice that once we hit the list of patriarchs whose names are more familiar to us—Abraham, Isaac, and Jacob, the three main patriarchs of the God of Israel—their ages start to decline considerably. Thus, Abraham is said to live to 175 (Genesis 25:7), Isaac to 180 (35:28-29), and Jacob to only 147 (47:28). Sarah is said to have died at 127 (23:1). More impressive is that Abraham's call by God to abandon his home and set out for the promised land came at age seventy-five (12:4)!

What are we to make of these incredible ages? Did they know some secret recipe for delaying old age that has been lost over time?

Unless you are really a biblical fundamentalist and take the Bible in every respect in a literal fashion, you obviously recognize that such figures are not meant to be taken literally. They are symbolic. They represent an extreme respect for growing old. Old age was equated with God's blessing and living an upright life. We must keep in mind that Genesis is the literature of myth. *Myth* does not mean falsehood. On the contrary, it means wrestling with deep truths. But these truths are couched in the form of stories and fantastic tales meant to promote appreciation of the universe from a religious, not scientific or historical, perspective. Myth is a category of literature. It is a way of reflecting deeply on the mysteries of the cosmos and human existence that find expression in narratives. So, these fantastic ages listed in Genesis are a way of acknowledging some of the heroes of ages past. They point to a mythical time when things seemed more perfect, and people lived more in tune with God's design. Old age is one of those distinguishing characteristics of Israel's heroes.

Old age is equated with God's blessing. The Book of Proverbs, for example, offers a common judgment: "Gray hair is a crown of glory; / it is gained in a righteous life" (Proverbs 16:31). An older translation of the same proverb uses a more poetic expression: "A hoary head is a crown of glory." Having a "hoary" head meant having gray or white hair; it was an expression for extreme old age. The term shows that such physical evidence is associated with having achieved something righteous in life and thus having been blessed by God. Old age counts for something.

Confirmation of this understanding (that exaggerating ages of important figures was a way of affirming age as venerable) is found in a comparable list of kings who ruled in Sumeria, a neighboring land in the ancient Near East. In a famous list of Sumerian kings they are said to have lived and ruled an even more fantastic number of years. For example, King Alulim ruled for 28,800 years; King Alalngar ruled for 36,000 years; King Enmenluana ruled for 43,200 years; and so on! By comparison, the distant patriarchs of Israel we listed above were quite short-lived.

A change in appreciation of old age, however, appears even in the Book of Genesis. After the earlier list of long-lived patriarchs, God seemingly decides to set a more reasonable time limit. "Then the LORD said, 'My spirit shall not abide in mortals forever, for they are flesh; their days shall be one hundred twenty years'" (Genesis 6:3). One hundred twenty years. That's still not a bad age limit. It's as if, all of a sudden, God decides that 120 years is a more acceptable time frame for human beings. A later book, Second Chronicles, says that one of the Jewish high priests in Israel's history, Jehoiada, lived to be 130, but again this is likely an exaggerated age to indicate the high esteem in which he was held. The author of Chronicles has a tendency to evaluate historical figures in simplistic terms of good and bad. In the case of this high priest, he is seen as good, and his age affirms his goodness. The praise heaped upon Jehoiada illustrates this judgment:

> They offered burnt offerings in the house of the LORD regularly all the days of Jehoiada.

> But Jehoiada grew old and full of days, and died; he was one hundred thirty years old at his death. And they buried him in the city of David among the kings, because he had done good in Israel, and for God and his house. (2 Chronicles 24:14-16)

Historical Perspective

At this point, we need to suspend the biblical viewpoint for a moment to ask what we really know from anthropology and archaeology about lifespans in the ancient world, including ancient Israel. In reality, there is no evidence whatsoever of such exaggerated advanced ages as the Bible recounts, despite what fundamentalists may tell you. These are clearly symbolic representations meant to honor distant ancestors. The reality was far different.

Historically speaking, in ancient Israel, the average lifespan was far less than it is today. Some scholars say that in Israel before the monarchy (tenth century BC), men and women both could only expect to live on average to the age of twenty-five or thirty![1] Others say it may have been as old as forty. That's a long way from even the 120-year limit of which Genesis speaks.

Men's lives could be shortened by very hard work, accident, plague, starvation (a periodic occurrence in years of drought and famine), or warfare. Women were threatened more by pregnancy and childbirth. (In fact, infant mortality itself was extremely high, which is why having a large number of children was desirable.) People also married much younger. Marriage (or at least engagement, which was tantamount to marriage) for a woman could be at age twelve, while men often married by age fifteen. If a man became a widower, he could often remarry and continue with his life. Women, on the other hand, if widowed, would have to find a male relative to marry them and protect them; otherwise they could expect to be marginalized in society and have their very survival up for grabs. This practice was called a levirate marriage (see Deuteronomy 25:5-6; from the Latin *levir*, "a husband's brother").

After the establishment of the monarchy, lifespans started to increase. Urbanization promoted better health. As cities grew, there was more security and more resources were on hand to promote longer life. Those who lived in rural contexts often faced the most challenges. They were threatened with tougher and shorter lives. We should also keep in mind that a study of fourteen kings in the Davidic line after King David shows that the average age was only forty-four.

The point is this: the biblical authors knew well that people's lives were basically very short—perhaps four decades at most. But there were always some exceptions to the rule. Some people, perhaps because of strong constitutions, good genes, or because they were more savvy about survival, lasted longer than others. The Bible itself establishes a norm for human lifespan. An anonymous psalmist writes: "The days of our life are seventy years, / or perhaps eighty, if we are strong; / even then their span is only toil and trouble; / they are soon gone, and we fly away" (Psalm 90:10).

With this text, we are getting a more down-to-earth perspective. If you lived to be seventy you were doing very well. Eighty meant you were even stronger than most. King David, Israel's most renowned king, was said to have lived to the age of seventy (2 Samuel 5:4). This would make him one of the exceptionally healthy adult males, but not extraordinary in his lifespan. St. Paul, centuries later, calls himself "an old man" (Philemon verse 9; Greek *presbytēs*), by which he means someone about age sixty. In fact, in New Testament times, sixty would be an advanced old age. I cite the Greek word used here because it is the same root as the word for "elder" (Greek *presbyteros* from which we get "presbyter" and "presbyterium") that the New Testament uses for distinguished community leaders. (More on this in chapter 3.)

Psalm 90 also reflects quite profoundly on our mortality with the following haunting words addressed to God:

> You turn us back to dust, / and say, "Turn back, you mortals." / For a thousand years in your sight / are like yesterday when it is past, / or like a watch in the night. / You sweep them away; they are like a dream, / like grass that is renewed in

the morning; / in the morning it flourishes and is renewed; / in the evening it fades and withers. (verses 3-6)

I think the psalmist's attitude here reflects what many people have experienced as they advance in age. Life is short. When we look at all the years that have constituted our life, do we not often ask: "Where did all those years go? How time flies!" Even worse is that the older we get the more quickly time seems to go. We can never outrun it. God's view of time is not the same as ours. As the author of Second Peter observes: "But do not ignore this one fact, beloved, that with the Lord one day is like a thousand years, and a thousand years are like one day" (3:8).

If God sees things from the perspective of eternity, we human beings can only comprehend what is in a normal lifespan, which today in fact has grown. In 1900 the lifespan of the average American was only forty-eight; in 1985 it was seventy-five; in 2015, the latest year for which data are available, it was about seventy-nine.[2] In other words, life expectancy continues to increase. Most people in Western cultures, barring illness or accident, can expect to live a rather long life. But living to 120 is still very rare.

A New Testament author, hundreds of years after the psalmist, expresses a similar attitude on the transitory character of life. In the context of warning people against an arrogant presumption that they are in charge of their life, the Letter of James says:

Come now, you who say, "Today or tomorrow we will go to such and such a town and spend a year there, doing business and making money." Yet you do not even know what tomorrow will bring. What is your life? For you are a mist that appears for a little while and then vanishes. Instead you ought to say, "If the Lord wishes, we will live and do this or that." (4:13-15)

Whether it be dust or mist, the message of the psalmist and of James is clear: that our life is ultimately fleeting. It is hard to "get hold of" in the sense of control. Living to a ripe old age, in fact, is not in everyone's future, as we well know from experience. Yet for many, it does arrive, and quicker than we expect.

Old Age in Modern Perspective

Several elderly people I have known over the years have said to me at times, as they lingered during an illness or simply from the fatigue of advanced years, how they wished God would take them home. For them old age—that is, their eighties or nineties—was becoming almost unbearable. They were ready to let go. They had looked over their life in retrospect and were willing to put their future in God's hands. They had no desire to live an inordinately long life. On the other hand, I know of a woman who, in her senior years, decided she wanted to live to be one hundred. She did just that, much to the surprise of her daughter and friends. And the next day she died. It was as if she had planned it all along, and it caused her family to marvel at her foresight.

Statistically, it is known that women tend to outlive men. This has been true for a very long time, and may be related to the need for men to work in physically demanding and dangerous occupations. But both women and men in modern times have lived extraordinarily long lives.[3] Nothing to compare with the ages in Genesis, of course, but impressive nonetheless. The oldest recorded and verifiable age of a human being was a French woman, Jeanne Calment, who lived for about 122 years, from 1875 to 1997. She allegedly had met the artist Vincent Van Gogh when she was just a schoolgirl. (In 2018, a scholar disputed her age and suggested she may have usurped her mother's birthdate, but this is uncertain.) The oldest known man, a Japanese man named Jiroemon Kimura, lived to more than 116 years. (Japan, in fact, has a record number of incredibly older people who remain quite active. One village is known for its high concentration of centenarians, though the secret of their longevity is not certain.)

As average ages globally continue to rise, especially as health care and nourishment improve in many areas of the world, questions about aging, its meaning, and its value are only going to increase. All the more reason we should examine the biblical teaching in more depth to see if there aren't choice bits of wisdom that will help us appreciate more deeply the phenomenon of growing old with dignity.

For Reflection:

- What pros and cons do you see in growing old? Do you see it as a blessing or a curse from God? Why?

- How well does modern society treat the elderly? Are there ways that our treatment of the elderly could be improved?

Chapter Two

Where Is the Fountain of Youth
When You Need It?

An elderly colleague of mine was fond of saying, "Youth is wasted on the young." He would then clarify what he meant. Wouldn't it be nice, he would say, if we had the same amount of experience and wisdom and prudence and judgment when we were young as we tend to have when we grow older? Who would not want to have the advantage of years of life experience while having the physical strength and stamina of a youth? Foolproof hindsight at age eighteen, perhaps? Alas, that is not the way of the world. As it is, some young people are wise beyond their years. Others, who are much older and should know better, do not always make the wisest choices in life. People can make mistakes and get themselves into trouble at any age.

Why is the ideal of youthfulness so attractive in our era? Conversely, why is growing old something generally looked down upon and something to be avoided? It is true that groups like the AARP, which began in 1958 as the American Association of Retired People, promote the benefits or advantages of old age. They are part of a larger movement for "gray power," as it was called in the 1970s.

They exist to "empower" people to choose how they wish to live as they age. Also, multiple types of residences for senior citizens have cropped up in the last few decades. Some are astonishingly elegant. They offer a range of care for the elderly, from independent living to assisted care to nursing care. My mother benefitted from one of these institutions. It was a blessing for our family to know that she was well cared for as she began her inevitable decline in health. So, there are numerous ways in which growing old in modern, Western, industrialized societies has become far more attractive. Yet, there remains a certain cultural emphasis on youthfulness.

One prominent influence on this attitude is modern media. Everywhere you look—magazines, newspapers, the Internet, television, cinema—the images that come across as attractive, dare we say "cool," are those that portray the vitality of youth. Advertisers slyly use good-looking, physically fit models to try to sell products that promise to bring back that youthful appearance, or put bounce back into your step. Unfortunately, some of the photos that accompany these slick ads are photo-shopped; no one looks that good! Women are particularly targeted by the advertising world, but men are hardly overlooked on the question of maintaining a youthful appearance. Commercials and advertisements announce the latest product promising to take away your wrinkles, smooth out that crepe-like skin, decrease your expanding waistline, and restore your energy. One recent ad boasted of a new youth "serum" guaranteed to keep you young and fit.

My elderly mother had a saying posted on her refrigerator that announced, "My get-up-and-go got up and went!" And she complained that the only way she could get through the day was to take a nap every afternoon. (Actually, some later data show that short daily naps might be beneficial to overall health.)

This modern obsession, in fact, is not entirely new. Ponce de León (1474-1521), first governor of Puerto Rico, famously set out in 1513 to find the legendary "fountain of youth." The legend goes back at least as far as the Greek historian Herodotus (fifth century BC), who spoke of a mythical natural spring in which bathers would find that their youth was restored. Following the tales told by indigenous peoples in the Caribbean, de León sailed to Florida. Little did he know that it would later be a haven for thousands of elderly retirees seeking the sun, the sea, and some diversion while awaiting their next developments. (I once overheard an acquaintance call Florida "God's waiting room"!)

Despite what advertisers want us to believe, there is no secret fountain of youth that is going to work its magic on us as we grow old. Yet we know there are things we can do to help us grow older in healthier ways. Good diet, regular exercise, sufficient sleep, and good family and friends are clearly assets to maintaining equilibrium in life as we age. But there is a connection between youth and age that we should explore, and the Bible has its own contribution to make to this issue.

The Ages of Human Beings

The first teaching to note in the Bible about aging is that it is *natural*. Aging is part of a seamless path that human beings usually follow, a continuum that extends from birth to death. The Book of Proverbs proclaims: "The glory of youths is their strength, / but the beauty of the aged is their gray hair" (20:29). The Bible, in fact, tends to speak of youth and old age in the same breath, contrasting and complementing them. If the young are valued for their vigor and vitality, the elderly are equally valued for their wisdom and insight. Of course, sometimes, youths are impetuous and arrogant, as in the case of Solomon's son Rehoboam who unwisely followed the counsel of the "young men" despite having consulted the wiser elders (1 Kings 12:6-11). But both approaches are recounted in the same story. Rehoboam's fate of losing half his kingdom to revolt shows the folly of not following the true wisdom of the elders, as the law recommends (Leviticus 19:32).

In a passage on rules governing votive offerings to God that people would make at various ages, the Book of Leviticus, which contains a large collection of laws for the people of Israel, is quite precise at naming distinctions.

> The LORD spoke to Moses, saying: Speak to the people of Israel and say to them: When a person makes an explicit vow to the LORD concerning the equivalent for a human being, the equivalent for a male shall be: from twenty to sixty years of age the equivalent shall be fifty shekels of

silver by the sanctuary shekel. If the person is a female, the equivalent is thirty shekels. If the age is from five to twenty years of age, the equivalent is twenty shekels for a male and ten shekels for a female. If the age is from one month to five years, the equivalent for a male is five shekels of silver, and for a female the equivalent is three shekels of silver. And if the person is sixty years old or over, then the equivalent for a male is fifteen shekels, and for a female ten shekels. If any cannot afford the equivalent, they shall be brought before the priest and the priest shall assess them; the priest shall assess them according to what each one making a vow can afford. (27:1-8)

What we should notice in this passage is that there are differences not only between ages but also sexes. Males and females were valued differently. In a highly patriarchal and hierarchical society such as ancient Israel, stereotypical roles developed that we might not consider appropriate today. Men were valued more than women because they had to protect the people, often by serving in battles. But women were still valued. They kept the home together, did much of the field work, and of course bore children and raised them.

This passage from Leviticus is also interesting for its concern for those who cannot afford the normal value of a votive offering. The priest is asked to make a judgment and demand only what the person can afford. As we know well, many elderly today live off fixed incomes. Some of these barely enable them to maintain a subsistence-level existence, let alone have money left over for more pleasurable activities. Old age and poverty, both in antiquity and today, are often linked.

The New Testament, surprisingly, does not have a whole lot to say about aging, though in later chapters we will see some nuances it brings to the topic. In the present context, we must note that some New Testament passages seemingly undervalue old age, at least metaphorically. For example, Jesus' contrast between new and old is instructive.

> No one sews a piece of unshrunk cloth on an old cloak; otherwise, the patch pulls away from it, the new from the old, and a worse tear is made. And no one puts new wine into old wineskins; otherwise, the wine will burst the skins, and the wine is lost, and so are the skins; but one puts new wine into fresh wineskins. (Mark 2:21-22)

The context of this passage, which has parallels in Matthew (9:16-17) and Luke (5:36-39), is a question Jesus is asked about why his disciples do not fast, as do the disciples of the Pharisees. Jesus' response is to explain in veiled terms that in the presence of the bridegroom (that is, himself), one does not fast but feast. When you are at a wedding, you do not hold back but indulge in the feasting. The teaching is part of a contrast between the newness of the gospel message and the "old" (Greek *palaios*) teaching that Jesus is now radicalizing with his talk of the kingdom of God. It does not downplay old people; it is simply a metaphor intended to contrast the gospel message with previous obligations.

Luke's version of this same saying, intriguingly, adds an important twist by means of Jesus' additional comment: "But new wine must be put into fresh wineskins. And no one after drinking old wine desires new wine, but says, 'The old is good'" (5:38-39). Here is a good insight indeed. Aged wine, as any wine lover can tell you, is infinitely better than young wine. Through the aging process—in barrels and bottles—the wine achieves a complexity, intensity, and quality that it would otherwise lack. In this case, aging is not only normal but preferable. For Luke, Jesus' teaching is not a rejection of the "old" but a fulfillment of it in a way, new and unexpected, which brings out the richness of the old. Again, however, the contrast is not about *persons* who are aging, but about the message Jesus brings.

Honor Your Father and Mother

Another aspect of the continuum between youth and old age is that they are ideally to be appreciative of one another. In the Ten Commandments, which most of us in the past had to learn by heart, we find the following instruction in the fourth commandment: "Honor your father and your mother" (Exodus 20:12; Deuteronomy 5:16). When I was a child and this commandment was drummed into my ears, I assumed naturally that it meant obeying my parents.

Why? Well, because they were my parents, and they were older and wiser.

In reality, this commandment is less about *children* obeying their parents than about reminding *adult children* to take care of their elderly parents. (Is it not true that no matter how old you are, you are always your parents' child?) That is the point of the commandment. Both in the Hebrew and Greek wording of the verb "honor," what is being commanded is an obligatory reverence and respect for one's elders. As they aged—and the same could be said today as in antiquity—the elderly were more vulnerable to exploitation. Thus, the commandment requires attentiveness to one's duty to watch over and care for one's parents, especially as they grow older. It was, and is, a weighty responsibility.

Elsewhere in the law there is a negative version of this same commandment, which we usually do not cite: "Whoever curses father or mother shall be put to death" (Exodus 21:17; also Leviticus 20:9). For obvious reasons, we do not emphasize this reverse version of the fourth commandment; capital punishment is a much more restricted reality today than it was in biblical times. (Most recently Pope Francis has spoken forcefully against it.) Yet the responsibility to care for elderly parents remains implicitly the same even in this warning.

In a bygone era, even as recently as the middle of the twentieth century, many adults ended up caring for elderly parents as they aged by taking them into their own home (or perhaps living with them in their house). As times have changed, and especially as more people live to a much more advanced age than ever before, it has become increasingly difficult to maintain this practice. Nowadays, more people end up in nursing homes, though at any given time, statistically, only about 5 percent of the elderly actually reside in nursing homes.

I can remember my parents taking care of my maternal grandmother in our house, though it was a hardship, and the house did not have a spare bedroom. Only when Grandma became too ill for my mother to care for her did she move to a nearby nursing home, where we could visit her on a regular basis. Given the pace and complexity of modern life, it is understandable that many adults cannot physically take care of their elderly parents in their own home. The case is even more difficult when the parent or parents suffer from a disability such as Alzheimer's disease, severe senility, or a serious illness that requires constant or intensive medical attention. The way the fourth commandment should echo in our ears, however, is in response to the question of how we are "honoring" our elderly. Hiding them in nursing homes where we can blithely ignore them, fail to visit them on a regular basis, or worse, just forget them, is clearly not what the fourth commandment intends.

Another book that teaches respect for parents is Sirach. Since it is found only in the Septuagint (the Greek translation of the Old Testament), Protestants do not consider it part of the canon of Sacred Scripture. It is part of the seven deuterocanonical (Greek, "second canon") works of the Bible, which Catholics do accept as part of the canon.

The title of the book comes from its author, Yeshua, son of Eleazar, son of Sira (= Ben Sira), a Jewish wisdom figure (sage) who lived in Jerusalem in the second century BC. His grandson translated the Hebrew version of the book into Greek in about 117 BC, and that is the only version that survives today. So we can consider the entire book a kind of testament to an old man's collected wisdom over his many years of experience. The grandson, moreover, added a preface to the book that gives many details about its author. What a nice way to honor his wise grandfather!

Catholics also call this book "Ecclesiasticus" (Latin, "church book") because it is filled with vital moral instruction and wisdom sayings that the Church has used in catechetical instruction through the ages. Many readings still appear in the Catholic Mass during the Church's liturgical year. Its advice is particularly down to earth and practical. As with most of the biblical wisdom literature, it offers a series of sayings that summarize good advice for women, men, children, and so on. On the need to "honor" one's father and "respect" one's mother, Sirach says:

> Do not glorify yourself by dishonoring your father, / for your father's dishonor is no glory to you. / The glory of one's father is one's own glory, / and it is a disgrace for children not to respect their mother. / My child, help your father in his old age, / and do not grieve him as long as

he lives; / even if his mind fails, be patient with him; / because you have all your faculties do not despise him. / For kindness to a father will not be forgotten, / and will be credited to you against your sins; / in the day of your distress it will be remembered in your favor; / like frost in fair weather, your sins will melt away. / Whoever forsakes a father is like a blasphemer, / and whoever angers a mother is cursed by the Lord. (3:10-16)

This passage most clearly exhibits the spirit of the fourth commandment. Adult children taking care of their parents as they grow older is a sacred obligation.

It is even more puzzling to see that in the New Testament, then, Jesus seems to downplay this important duty. Jesus cites the fourth commandment in response to a question about observing the commandments.

You know the commandments: "You shall not murder; You shall not commit adultery; You shall not steal; You shall not bear false witness; You shall not defraud; Honor your father and mother." (Mark 10:19)

His questioner responds that he has kept all these, which Jesus affirms, but he then goes on to invite the man to leave everything to follow him (Mark 10:20-22; also Matthew 19:16-22). Noteworthy is that in Matthew's version of this story, the one posing the question is called a "young man" (Greek *neaniskos*, "youth"; Matthew 19:22), which can mean someone between the ages of twenty-four and forty. This tends to heighten the responsibility he has to take care of his elderly parents.

But in another passage Jesus does something startling. He advises a would-be disciple to follow him *immediately*, even to the point of ignoring the sacred obligation to bury his elderly father. Jesus almost seems to be insensitive: "Another of his disciples said to him, 'Lord, first let me go and bury my father.' But Jesus said to him, 'Follow me, and let the dead bury their own dead'" (Matthew 8:21-22; see also Luke 9:59-60). How could he advise this individual to ignore his moral obligation to see that his father is properly buried? At first glance, Jesus' demand may seem harsh. It seems to minimize the requirements of the Jewish Law. It is not meant in that way, however. To understand this Gospel passage, we need to place it in context. Jesus is not proposing that the man violate the fourth commandment. Rather, he is showing that his call for disciples to "follow" him and to proclaim the good news (gospel message) of the kingdom is more urgent, more demanding, and more critical at this time than even the profound obligation to take care of one's elderly parents, even including providing for their proper burial (Tobit 4:3-4).

Turning Back the Clock

I once heard a joke that went something like this. A man named Marvin was upset that he was growing old. So, he decided to do something about it. He went to a hairstylist and dyed his hair to remove all the gray. Then he went to a dentist and had all his rotting teeth replaced with nice pearly whites. He then saw a plastic surgeon who did a tummy-tuck, removed the lines around his eyes, and administered Botox to smooth out the wrinkles in his face. Finally, he started going to a spa where he began to exercise and to eat healthy foods, and overall tried to reform his lifestyle. Shortly thereafter, while leaving the spa one afternoon, he was crossing the street when a speeding car came out of nowhere and hit him, killing him instantly. Marvin arrived at the pearly gates of heaven where he encountered none other than God. Immediately, Marvin launched into a tirade. He cried out, "Why did you do that, Lord? Why did you let me die when I was just getting my act together?" Out came the unexpected response: "Honest, Marvin, I didn't recognize you!"

This humorous story makes no sense on one level, yet it contains a little kernel of truth. All our modern attempts to delay old age, to turn back the clock, to hold decrepitude at bay will amount to nothing. The clock stops for no one.

In antiquity, as we have seen thus far in this book, old age was taken for granted. It is part and parcel of human existence. It is good that modern Western people have grown more conscious of the need for healthier lifestyles, but that alone is not the response to old age. All our cosmetic surgery and fancy drugs are futile in the long run.

One of the Fathers of the Church who was also a renowned theologian, Clement of Alexandria (died ca. AD

214), would certainly not be welcomed in the plastic surgery salons of Los Angeles. He spoke out boldly in his day to discourage the dyeing of one's hair in order to disguise aging.[4] He claimed:

> "For they think, that like serpents they divest themselves of the old age of their head by painting and renovating themselves. But though they do doctor the hair cleverly, they will not escape wrinkles, nor will they elude death by tricking time."

In the same passage, he goes on to reaffirm the value of old age: "The more, then, a man hastes to the end, the more truly venerable is he, having God alone as his senior, since He is the eternal aged One, He who is older than all things." So, despite our desires otherwise, the fountain of youth is an illusion. We should probably just accept this reality.

For Reflection:

- What do you think is the secret of staying young, or at least "young at heart"? Do you believe aging can be delayed? Altered? Why or why not?

- Recall older people you know. What do you most admire about them? What are the traits they possess that are worth imitating? What aspects of their lives are less attractive?

Chapter Three

Experience Equals Wisdom ... Or Does It?

When I was a new faculty member of a seminary many years ago, I regularly sat beside an older, more experienced colleague. He would occasionally bend toward me to help interpret one intervention or another so that I could "learn the ropes," as the saying goes. I sensed that, as a young priest and totally new at seminary formation ministry, I should hold my tongue and learn from my wiser elders at the table. In hindsight, I still think that was good advice. I did indeed learn a lot in those days that I was later able to put to use.

But one day, he startled me. One of the faculty members was going on at some length about his long experience in priestly formation. My neighbor suddenly leaned toward me and whispered, "Remember, sometimes experience is nothing but old ignorance!" I almost burst out laughing. Later, I asked him to explain a bit more what he meant. He told me it was something that had been passed on to him by an older colleague, long deceased. He explained that sometimes the elderly take refuge in the idea that their long experience over time alone gives them the right to make pronouncements about wisdom from the ages. It's as if experience trumps everything. But sometimes, he found, their so-called wisdom was nothing more than the inability or anxiety to try new ideas, to go new directions, or to learn something totally new. He discovered that some older faculty members had a tendency to dismiss any new suggestion of ways to do things differently, just because it was different, and perhaps also because the suggestion came from a newer, younger member of the faculty.

You have no doubt heard the saying: "You can't teach an old dog new tricks." There is some truth to this adage. Sometimes seniors prefer to resist any kind of novelty because it will involve change. It is far more comfortable to use tried and true methods than to risk attempting something novel. Many elderly people do not tolerate change well, especially when it comes to their personal schedules or habits. There is also a natural fear of the unknown and the unfamiliar.

There is another side to this coin, however. Sometimes older people can astonish us. They are the source of much novelty. Their inventiveness, their creativity, their ability to see with fresh eyes sometimes surprise us. Once in a while even their energy and capacity to endure astonish. Let's take just a few examples from human history.

Leonardo da Vinci, who was a brilliant artist and inventor at an early age, went on to accomplish many of his most notable works when he was elderly. Catherine the Great, who was empress of Russia for some thirty-four years in the eighteenth century, ruled with intelligence and foresight, enabling Russia to become a world power at the time. Queen Victoria dominated the United Kingdom throughout much of the nineteenth century, ruling Britain for more than sixty-three years with brilliance and vitality, despite the restrictions of that era, which undervalued the role of women in society. Ironically, she gave the era its name—the Victorian Era. She was only recently surpassed by Queen Elizabeth II of the United Kingdom, who now, at age ninety-two, holds the record for the world's longest-reigning current monarch—and whose energy seems never to diminish. Winston Churchill was considered an elderly statesman when he was called upon to lead Great Britain in the midst of World War II. He went on to inspire his nation—with the help of the Allies, of course—to victory. Pablo Picasso not only did some of his most famous, controversial, and innovative works as he grew older, but he fathered a child when he was in his eighties. Each of these individuals is memorable for what they achieved in their "dotage"! One could multiply the examples. The fact is that many elderly people throughout history marked their era with incredible accomplishments that women and men of far younger ages could scarcely imagine.

Biblical Examples

The Bible also has something to contribute to this understanding. It is no exaggeration to say that the Bible basically equates age with wisdom. Multiple passages attest to this assertion. First, however, we should recall that the Bible speaks of old age by the image of "gray hair." The

Book of Proverbs, for instance, asserts that "Gray hair is a crown of glory; / it is gained in a righteous life" (Proverbs 16:31). The Book of Wisdom makes the explicit connection between gray hair and wisdom: "For old age is not honored for length of time, / or measured by number of years; / but understanding is gray hair for anyone, / and a blameless life is ripe old age" (4:8-9).

The old sage Ben Sira, whose grandson, as we saw earlier, collected his teachings and organized them in a book, also gives explicit advice to the young to seek the wisdom which comes with age. "My child, from your youth choose discipline, / and when you have gray hair you will still find wisdom" (Sirach 6:18). Here we should recall that the goal of all wisdom literature in the Bible was to instruct young men on the proper ways of assuming their adult duties. It constituted wise advice from the sages to youth.

The expression "gray hair" (Hebrew *sēbah*), in fact, means "woolly head," with an allusion to the wool of sheep. Having gray, white, or woolly hair (Old English "hoary") is a virtual synonym for being old and wise. In one passage describing the death of Gideon, the Hebrew word used for a "good old age" is *sēbah*, literally "woolly hair": "Then Gideon son of Joash died at a good old age, and was buried in the tomb of his father Joash at Ophrah of the Abiezrites" (Judges 8:32). The very same expression is used for King David's death: "He died in a good old age, full of days, riches, and honor; and his son Solomon succeeded him" (1 Chronicles 29:28).

Curiously, perhaps, although baldness is clearly known in the Bible, it is not equated with wisdom as gray hair is. According to some ancient traditions, St. Paul is said to have been bald,[5] and in one of his last extant letters he calls himself "an old man" (Philemon verse 9). But the lack of hair on his head is not identified with any particular wisdom or insight. That comes rather from the force of his teaching and his letters.

A further comment on baldness is worth noting here. Although some forms of baldness in the Bible are associated with skin diseases, and thus considered "unclean" in the biblical categories of cultic cleanness and uncleanness, baldness itself is simply noted as a human condition for some people. "If anyone loses the hair from his head, he is bald but he is clean. If he loses the hair from his forehead and temples, he has baldness of the forehead but he is clean" (Leviticus 13:40-41). The revised New American Bible translation makes the first verse of this passage even clearer: "When a man loses the hair of his head, he is simply bald on the crown and not unclean" (Leviticus 13:40, NABRE). To tell the truth, I am comforted by this verse! It is a relief to know that hair loss is not simply a modern phenomenon, nor a sign of some debilitating condition.

Under certain circumstances, baldness, or totally shaving off one's hair, could be an indication of something other than age. It can be a sign of mourning (Jeremiah 16:6; Ezekiel 27:31; Micah 1:16), repentance (Isaiah 22:12), or of being defeated (Isaiah 15:2-3). The eighth-century-BC prophet Micah, foreseeing disaster for Judah, exhibits a familiar attitude with regard to the experience of the exile. He poignantly exhorts: "Make yourselves bald and cut off your hair / for your pampered children; / make yourselves as bald as the eagle, / for they have gone from you into exile" (Micah 1:16). One other case of voluntary baldness is when either men or women shaved their heads in order to take an oath called the "nazirite vow" (Numbers 6:2, 18). St. Paul seems to have done this on at least one occasion, although the nature of his vow is not clearly explained. Acts says simply: "At Cenchreae [one of the ports of Corinth] he had his hair cut, for he was under a vow" (Acts 18:18). In any case, in contrast to gray hair, these instances show us that baldness is not connected with wisdom. (I say this with sincere apologies to my Uncle John who will likely be upset with me to hear this. He has been bald since he was a young man, and is fond of defending it by saying, "Grass does not grow on a busy street!" He has always been wise in my eyes.)

Elders in the Community

One of the ways in which the Bible reinforces the connection between age and wisdom is in the position of the "elders" (Hebrew *zaqēn*). These figures are present in both the Old and New Testaments. We would not be exaggerating to call the type of government found in biblical times a gerontocracy (from Greek *gēron*, "old"), a group of old men. Modern governments have sometimes continued the same tendency! In Latin, the word "elder" is *senator*, and in the Roman republic the senate was indeed a group of old men whose job was to manage many aspects of Roman life. They constituted the Senate; they were the elder statesmen, usually of aristocratic or upper middle class standing, who had stature and wealth in the community.

In the Old Testament, the word "elders" is used of various leaders at different times in Israel's history. They are mentioned hundreds of times, and in different periods they functioned as leaders and government officials on various levels. Thus there are the "elders of Israel" who are to represent the Israelites to the pharaoh in Egypt and basically lobby on their behalf (Exodus 3:16,18). They help Moses and Aaron keep the people informed of God's will (Exodus 4:29). Individual towns also had elders, local leaders who enforced various laws and practices among the people (Deuteronomy 21:3-4, 25:8).

At times, there seems to be a distinction between the elders and the judges, those who led the people of Israel before the establishment of the monarchy (Joshua 24:1). One of the functions of such leaders may have been in discerning court cases, which were conducted at the city gates. Thus some passages literally refer to the "elders at the gate" (Deuteronomy 25:7). Another function may have been at the liturgy in the Temple, since some passages refer to "elders of the congregation." This expression seems to imply some role in sacrificial offerings (Leviticus 4:15; Judges 21:16). What unites all these different elders is that they occupied a leadership role by virtue of their age and wisdom. (Keeping in mind the patriarchal orientation of ancient Israel, we see that women are usually left out of this perspective, but not always. Deborah, for instance, is one of the judges and is also called a prophet [Judges 4:4].)

In the New Testament, we must distinguish two kinds of elders. The most easily identifiable are the elders among the Jewish leaders in Jerusalem. They are identified with the chief priests and scribes who constitute the Jewish opposition to Jesus and his teaching, according to the Gospels (Matthew 16:21; Mark 11:27; Luke 20:1; John 8:9). In the Acts of the Apostles, it is the "whole council of [Jewish] elders" whom Paul says gave him authority to go to Damascus to arrest followers of Christ prior to his conversion (Acts 22:5). All of these references are to some authorities within Judaism. Lest we conclude that this means all Jews were opposed to Christians—a concept that comes only later in the tradition—we must remember that the earliest Christians were Jews themselves. Jesus and all his apostles were Jews. Saul, later known as Paul, was born a Jew, lived as a Jew, and died as a Jew, albeit one who accepted Jesus as the long-awaited messiah. The differences that emerged, which eventually led to a parting of the ways between Jews and Christians, came later. Unfortunately these also led to unacceptable anti-Jewish and anti-Semitic actions that are not supported by Gospel texts.

A second kind of elder is also apparent in the New Testament. The early Christians themselves adopted some of the same leadership structure with which they were familiar in Judaism. So we find references to elders (*presbyteroi*) in some passages that refer to specifically Christian leaders.

We see, for instance, Paul giving his younger colleague Timothy advice: "Do not neglect the gift that is in you, which was given to you through prophecy with the laying on of hands by the council of elders" (1 Timothy 4:14). In the same letter, the elders are praised with the following words: "Let the elders who rule well be considered worthy of double honor, especially those who labor in preaching and teaching" (5:17). Paul also warns against being too quick to make judgments against an elder. "Never accept any accusation against an elder except on the evidence of two or three witnesses" (5:19). It is as if one should tread carefully and be sure to have one's facts straight, with corroboration, before accusing an elder of some mistake.

The Letter of James mentions "elders of the church" who are called upon to pray over the sick (James 5:14), indicating that they also had some function in liturgical or sacramental matters. The author of two of the Letters of John calls himself an "elder" (2 John 1:1; 3 John 1:1), as does the author of the First Letter of Peter (1 Peter 5:1). Exactly what these designations mean for the early Church, however, is not clear in the New Testament. What seems apparent is that the early Church followed the Jewish custom of looking to "elders" to serve in leadership positions, most likely because they were considered trustworthy, experienced, and wise.

In the Pastoral Letters (First and Second Timothy and Titus), several passages use the Greek word for elders (*presbyteroi*) in connection with the Greek expressions "overseers" (*episkopoi*) and "servants" (*diakonoi*). Later in Church history, these three offices evolved into the three separate ordained ministries of bishop, priest, and deacon. However, in the New Testament period the roles of the elders and overseers appear to have been intermingled (Philippians 1:1). Thus Christian leadership centered around two main roles, elders and deacons, though other leadership roles are also evident. In Acts, the elders are designated a distinct group, as are the apostles (Acts 15:4, 6, 22-23). Once more, though, distinct duties are not described other than some sort of leadership position.

With regard to Christian elders as associated with age, we should exercise some caution. Timothy, for instance, is a much younger colleague to Paul, and yet he is clearly in a leadership role with Paul's blessing. In the early Church, leadership was associated with giftedness and the capacity to exercise authority, not simply with age. It is true, nonetheless, that the same respect seen in the Old Testament for elders in the community is also evident in New Testament communities.

Wisdom and Age

So far, we have been exploring the connection between old age and leadership or authority. We need a bit more nuance, however. The Bible does not always associate wisdom with old age. Wisdom can come to anyone at any age if he or she is open to God's will. Let's examine a few passages. The Book of Wisdom, for instance, expresses this view:

But the righteous, though they die early, will be at rest. / For old age is not honored for length of time, / or measured by number of years; / but understanding is gray hair for anyone, / and a blameless life is ripe old age. (4:7-9)

What this text says is that living a righteous life is more important than living a *long* life. It is not the length of one's life that counts, but the quality. Furthermore, "understanding" (wisdom) is identified with "gray hair for anyone." This text subtly recognizes that true wisdom, often identified with "gray hairs," can be found at any age.

A similar text is found in another wisdom book, Sirach.

Three kinds of people I hate, / and I loathe their manner of life: / A proud pauper, a rich liar, / and a lecherous old fool. / In your youth you did not gather. / How will you find anything in your old age? / How appropriate is sound judgment in the gray-haired, / and good counsel in the elderly! / How appropriate is wisdom in the aged, / understanding and counsel in the venerable! / The crown of the elderly, wide experience; / their glory, the fear of the Lord. (25:2-6, NABRE)

Sirach, in fact is a good example of why wisdom should be sought when one is young. In the last chapter of his book, he testifies to having sought wisdom his whole life long. Now that he is old and has chosen to write down his life experience, he summarizes his life succinctly.

While I was still young, before I went on my travels, / I sought wisdom openly in my prayer. / Before the temple I asked for her, / and I will search for her until the end. / From the first blossom to the ripening grape / my heart delighted in her; / my foot walked on the straight path; / from my youth I followed her steps. / I inclined my ear a little and received her, / and I found for myself much instruction. (51:13-16)

We should not miss an aspect of Sirach's teaching that is striking and that is characteristic of the entire Old Testament. He personifies wisdom as a woman! Despite Israel's persistent orientation toward male dominance, it is the "Wisdom Woman" who is to be sought. She is the source of truth, righteousness, and knowledge. His praise for her knows no bounds. He continues:

My soul grappled with wisdom, / and in my conduct I was strict; / I spread out my hands to the heavens, / and lamented my ignorance of her. / I directed my soul to her, / and in purity I found her. / With her I gained understanding from the first; / therefore I will never be forsaken. / My heart was stirred to seek her; / therefore I have gained a prize possession. (51:19-21)

What such passages show us is that wisdom was a value to be sought by the young but that often only arrived in its full stature with age and experience. The whole wisdom tradition of the Bible is oriented toward this goal of instructing young men to seek the Wisdom Woman. She can become their lifelong companion.

In the next chapter, we will take a look at the implications of what happens when such traditional wisdom is turned on its head.

For Reflection:

- How do you correlate wisdom with age? Do you believe most people acquire wisdom as they grow older? If not, what might prevent such a development?

- Who are the "elders" in communities you know? Do they deserve this designation? Do they truly represent collective wisdom that affirms our confidence in their leadership?

Chapter Four

When the Tables are Turned: The Wisdom of Youth vs. the Wisdom of the Aged

What we have seen thus far is that frequently, the Bible testifies to the belief that wisdom is often found in the aged, even if it is learned earlier in life. But what happens when the tables are turned?

A few years ago I remember reading a newspaper article that announced in bold letters the election of a new mayor in some small town in rural America. The article proclaimed what an upset had happened in this election because the victor was only eighteen years old! He was just old enough to vote, and he won the election by defeating a much older incumbent. I had to ask myself: Is this young man really old or experienced enough to be mayor? Even of a very small town? I have no idea what ultimately happened thereafter. Maybe it was a disastrous experiment that went down in flames. Or perhaps he actually did the town some good. What the event showed, however, is that sometimes, despite tendencies to the contrary, people will go with a younger, newer face. It can challenge the wisdom of the aged.

There is something in the American spirit that loves an underdog. Many films (especially animated ones), in fact, take up the theme of the unknown, unsuspecting young woman or man who has a secret destiny to save their civilization or achieve some monumental task that no one else had heretofore been able to do. Sometimes there is more wisdom in the young than we could ever have imagined.

There are countless tales of how young heroes overcome the machinations of older but more devious individuals. In such instances, we might say that the tables have been turned upside down. The ones you thought should be wise, honest, and upright turn out to be twisted and out to get whatever they can. Sometimes, too, the young, whom you would expect not to have the experience, or perhaps the necessary deep-rooted sense of justice, are the ones who "save the day." Let's look at one prominent example from the Bible.

The Story of Susanna and the Elders

Perhaps the classic biblical illustration of the theme of "dirty old men" is the story of Susanna and the elders in the Book of Daniel. We need to preface this story with a comment, though.

Although this addition to Daniel was likely written in Hebrew or Aramaic (a related Semitic language), it is not found in the Hebrew Bible. Rather, it exists only in a Greek version of the Old Testament (called the Septuagint [abbreviated with the Roman numeral for "70," LXX]) that the Jews preserved in the diaspora, that is, outside of the Holy Land. The Catholic Church has always regarded the Septuagint, which contains seven more books than the Hebrew Bible, as canonical Scripture, although Protestants do not. They are even used for readings at Mass on occasion. The seven are: Judith, Tobit, Baruch, Wisdom (also called the Wisdom of Solomon), Sirach (also called Ben Sira or Ecclesiasticus), and First and Second Maccabees. In addition, there are more chapters in the books of Esther and Daniel.

The story of Susanna is one of the stories found in the Greek manuscript of Daniel (13:1-64). It has delighted people through the ages, for it is like an ancient detective story, describing a near miscarriage of justice against an innocent young woman because of two lecherous old men.

Susanna, a beautiful Jewish woman in Babylon (where the Jews were exiled in the seventh century BC), is called a "God-fearing woman." She marries a rich Jewish man named Joakim whose luxurious house had a garden where Susanna liked to bathe on warm days. Two old men who serve as "judges" see her regularly going into the garden and lust after her. Then the plot thickens.

> Once, while [the elders] were watching for an opportune day, she went in as before with only two maids, and wished to bathe in the garden, for it was a hot day. No one was there except the two elders, who had hidden themselves and were watching her. She said to her maids, "Bring

me olive oil and ointments, and shut the garden doors so that I can bathe." They did as she told them: they shut the doors of the garden and went out by the side doors to bring what they had been commanded; they did not see the elders, because they were hiding.

When the maids had gone out, the two elders got up and ran to her. They said, "Look, the garden doors are shut, and no one can see us. We are burning with desire for you; so give your consent, and lie with us. If you refuse, we will testify against you that a young man was with you, and this was why you sent your maids away." (verses 15-21)

Susanna realizes she is trapped. She is a lone woman in a patriarchal society. She has two strikes against her. First, a woman's testimony counted for little, and second, the two old men are respected leaders. Not only do they hold positions of power, but they could corroborate one another's false testimony (in accordance with the rule in Deuteronomy 19:15) and thus have the young woman condemned as a harlot. Nonetheless, the story continues, Susanna decides it is better to scream for help and face the consequences than tarnish her marriage and "sin in the sight of the Lord" (verse 23).

Then Susanna cried out with a loud voice, and the two elders shouted against her. And one of them ran and opened the garden doors. When the people in the house heard the shouting in the garden, they rushed in at the side door to see what had happened to her. And when the elders told their story, the servants felt very much ashamed, for nothing like this had ever been said about Susanna. (verses 24-27)

Susanna is indeed cornered, and the two scoundrels proceed with accusations that Susanna was caught in the act of adultery, a crime punishable by death.

Enter a young hero, the prophet Daniel. Surprisingly, the elders of the court invite the young man Daniel to take charge of the trial after he protests the injustice, saying to him: "'Come, sit with us and inform us, since God has given you the prestige of old age.' But he replied, 'Separate these two far from one another, and I will examine them'" (verses 50-51, NABRE). Notice how the view of the elderly as possessing good judgment is here upheld. The town elders attribute to the young man wisdom beyond his age. Yet a paradox is also evident. The lecherous old men who should be righteous and wise will be shown to be perverse, while the young man will exhibit true wisdom.

As the tale unwinds, Daniel questions the two old men separately, accusing one of being "an old relic of wicked days" (verse 52), and asserting of the other that "beauty has beguiled you and lust has perverted your heart" (verse 56). He asks each of them separately under what kind of tree they had discovered Susanna with her alleged suitor.

One claims it was a "mastic tree" (verse 54) while the other says it was an "evergreen oak" (verse 58). Their cruel lie is unmasked, and the assembled citizens react in fury.

> Then the whole assembly raised a great shout and blessed God, who saves those who hope in him. And they took action against the two elders, because out of their own mouths Daniel had convicted them of bearing false witness; they did to them as they had wickedly planned to do to their neighbor. Acting in accordance with the law of Moses, they put them to death. Thus innocent blood was spared that day. (verses 60-62)

In the end, the two old lechers pay for their crime, Susanna's honor is upheld, and Daniel's reputation as a wise prophet beyond his years expands.

It was worth recounting this story at length, for it shows that in old age, lustful desires can lead people into serious sinfulness. Moreover, the story provides evidence that even in biblical times, sexual desire did not necessarily disappear with old age. The Bible also does not tolerate sexual immorality at any age (Sirach 42:8), nor do the aged get away with evil deeds just because of their age (1 Kings 2:6-9). More importantly, though, this story shows that the young can sometimes surprisingly be the source of great inspiration. They can turn out to have greater moral depth and perception than their elders.

Wisdom and Boldness

I conclude this chapter with another biblical example. In this case, it shows a situation where perhaps only a senior could "get away with it" by acting boldly.

One of the more fascinating stories in the Old Testament is Abraham's intercession on behalf of the sinful city of Sodom (Genesis 18:16-33). The context is clear that Abraham is already elderly, as it comes after God's promise to make him fertile, despite his old age (18:12). God deplores the sad state of sinfulness in Sodom and vows to destroy it. But suddenly, Abraham revs up his courage and boldly confronts God.

> "Will you indeed sweep away the righteous with the wicked? Suppose there are fifty righteous within the city; will you then sweep away the place and not forgive it for the fifty righteous who are in it? Far be it from you to do such a thing, to slay the righteous with the wicked, so that the righteous fare as the wicked! Far be that from you! Shall not the Judge of all the earth do what is just?" And the LORD said, "If I find at Sodom fifty righteous in the city, I will forgive the whole place for their sake." Abraham answered, "Let me take it upon myself to speak to the Lord, I who am but dust and ashes. Suppose five of the fifty righteous are lacking? Will you destroy the whole city for lack of five?" And he said, "I will not destroy it if I find forty-five there." (Genesis 18:23-28)

This is surely cheeky on Abraham's part. But the story continues. Abraham keeps bargaining with God, whittling away at the numbers whom God will destroy. God relents at forty, then thirty, then twenty, until we arrive at the last exchange.

> Then [Abraham] said, "Oh do not let the Lord be angry if I speak just once more. Suppose ten are found there." He answered, "For the sake of ten I will not destroy it."

> And the LORD went his way, when he had finished speaking to Abraham; and Abraham returned to his place. (18:32-33)

At this point, one has to wonder if God was rolling his eyes. Had Abraham finally worn down the Lord? The story, of course, says more about God's mercy than it does about Abraham's bold manner. Yet I cannot help but think that it is a tale that makes sense in the context of old age. Abraham had already had considerable experience with God, and God had promised to act favorably toward him by giving him progeny. What emboldened Abraham to intervene on behalf of a wicked city? Was it concern for the innocent residents who would perish along with the guilty? Or does he think he has some special "in" with God that will enable him to bargain? Does his special friendship with God embolden him to test the extent of God's mercy? Or is he just pressing his luck? At the very least, the tale shows that the elderly can sometimes act in an impressively wily fashion. Perhaps he had little to lose, given his age. Or perhaps he thought his friendship with God, the Lord of heaven and earth, would warrant greater tolerance of his cheekiness. Or maybe he had simply become more courageous. In any event, I wonder whether a younger individual could have achieved the same result.

For Reflection:

- Can you think of any instances where the elderly were outperformed by more youthful adversaries (apart from athletic contests, of course)? How do you perceive such events? Do they tarnish your view of the elderly?

- Ideally, how do you think the elderly and younger people should interact? What constitutes *wisdom* with regard to the human person?

Chapter Five

It's Not *That* You Grow Old, But *How*

Have you ever looked in the mirror and wondered, "Who is that person staring back at me?" I fear that most of us, as we grow older, have similar experiences where suddenly we grow conscious of our increasing age and diminishing capacities. It can be difficult to accept that, as time marches on, we change. We shrink in height and grow in width. We get more and more wrinkles, and our eyesight and hearing tend to be impaired in one way or another. The inevitable march of time takes its toll to such a degree that we barely recognize ourselves.

Anyone who has encountered senior citizens knows well the catalogue of complaints that accompany old age. One's stamina is not the same. In addition to fatigue, poor eyesight, and poor hearing, one's taste buds lose the ability to entice one's appetite. Joints ache. Incontinence and constipation can set in. One spends more time setting up and attending medical appointments than just about anything else. The list could go on. Lest we think this experience is a modern reality without parallel in antiquity, we need to take a look at some ancient testimony which might be surprising.

Ancient Perspectives on Old Age

One time many years ago while reading a biography of St. Jerome, I stumbled on a passage that took my breath away. It was almost modern in perspective. St. Jerome obviously lived after the events of the Bible (in the fourth century AD); he was perhaps the greatest biblical scholar of his era, and he had an enduring impact on biblical interpretation throughout history. But Jerome was a curmudgeon. He had a temper, and as he grew older, he got more and more cantankerous. His modern biographer was struck by a lengthy passage in one of Jerome's letters where he reflected on aging. I quote the passage at length because it is a marvelous summary of Jerome's personality as he grew older.

> In one eloquent paragraph Jerome paints what must surely (even allowing for exaggerations of conventional rhetoric) be a portrait of himself, now in his middle seventies and ruefully conscious of his years—a portrait, moreover, which for a moment lays bare his guilt–ridden psychology. Old age, he muses, brings with it both blessings and misfortunes. It is to be welcomed because it liberates one from the dominance of shameful pleasures, sets bounds to gluttony, breaks the onset of lust, bestows enhanced wisdom, a more mature good sense. As the bodily organism grows chill, one is glad to leave sensual enjoyments to younger people. On the debit side,

however, must be set frequent illnesses, disgusting phlegm, fading eyesight, digestive acidity, trembling hands, gums receding from the teeth, and the teeth themselves dropping out as one eats. On top of all this one is the victim of griping stomach pains, gout in the feet and arthritis in the hands, so that holding a pen to write and walking on one's own feet are well-nigh impossible. Whole parts of one's body seem already dead. Then, after this terrifying catalogue, he adds with relief: "In spite of all this, in making my choice of misfortunes I shall the more readily put up with illnesses provided I am released from that uniquely burdensome tyrant, sexual desire."[6]

This excerpt reveals Jerome's complex psychological makeup. He was a priest and also the founder of a monastic community in Jerusalem where he went to work in seclusion on his famous Latin translation of the Bible, the Vulgate. Yet he was clearly troubled by sexual desire, which he felt finally diminished in old age, for which he was grateful. (I am not sure Jerome is alone in being troubled by sexual desire in old age! He may have been particularly bothered by his urges, but many elderly people, I suspect, remain troubled or perplexed by similar desires, even in a diminished state.) What is intriguing in this summary passage is that he captures the experience of so many people about the realities of growing older. Notice that there is some balance in his summation. There are positives and negatives. On the positive side are more moderation in life, more wisdom, and more good sense. On the negative side comes the catalogue of physical debilities which so frequently accompany old age.

Further Biblical Insights on Old Age

These experiences of diminishing capacity in old age are not new. They even date before St. Jerome. The Bible itself provides some indication of the same phenomena. For example, in old age, Isaac is said to have had poor eyesight (Genesis 27:1, 48:10), as did Ahijah (1 Kings 14:4). The psalmist acknowledges diminishment of strength in old age (Psalm 71:9) and also pleads with God not to abandon him in his dotage (verse 18). Even gout is mentioned in the Bible as a "disease of the feet" in old age, an affliction suffered by King Asa (1 Kings 15:23).

There is also a fascinating portrayal of King David in his old age ("very old" according to 1 Kings 1:15) that shows that the ancients were well aware of the physical ravages age brings upon someone. In this instance, David constantly feels cold, perhaps owing to poor circulation.

> King David was old and advanced in years; and although they covered him with clothes, he could not get warm. So his servants said to him, "Let a young virgin be sought for my lord the king, and let her wait on the king, and be his attendant; let her lie in your bosom, so that my lord the king may be warm." So they searched for a beautiful girl

throughout all the territory of Israel, and found Abishag the Shunammite, and brought her to the king. The girl was very beautiful. She became the king's attendant and served him, but the king did not know her sexually. (1 Kings 1:1-4)

One has to wonder that the "remedy" for David's condition would be a young virgin to keep him warm, given his earlier adultery with Bathsheba! But David, whether for lack of desire or capacity, or perhaps for his reformed ethical stance, resists having sexual relations with her.

Another classic example is in Qoheleth (also called the Book of Ecclesiastes), whose title means "the Preacher." Writing to younger people, he gives some sage advice as he catalogues the typical complaints of old age.

Remember your creator in the days of your youth, before the days of trouble come, and the years draw near when you will say, "I have no pleasure in them"; before the sun and the light and the moon and the stars are darkened and the clouds return with the rain; in the day when the guards of the house tremble, and the strong men are bent, and the women who grind cease working because they are few, and those who look through the windows see dimly; when the doors on the street are shut, and the sound of the grinding is low, and one rises up at the sound of a bird, and all the daughters of song are brought low; when one is afraid of heights, and terrors are in the road; the almond tree blossoms, the grasshopper drags itself along and desire fails; because all must go to their eternal home, and the mourners will go about the streets; before the silver cord is snapped, and the golden bowl is broken, and the pitcher is broken at the fountain, and the wheel broken at the cistern, and the dust returns to the earth as it was, and the breath returns to God who gave it. (Ecclesiastes 12:1-7)

We should remember, of course, that Qoheleth is the stubborn, pessimistic skeptic of the Old Testament. He's an original complainer. He sees the proverbial cup half empty rather than half full. Not someone to read when you are in a depressed mood. Yet his book of wisdom sayings is preserved in the canon surely because it offers some wise and true advice.

Old age is not all downhill, however. The Bible also speaks of seniors who flourished in their old age, and who continued to make an impact. One example is Moses. The Book of Deuteronomy says of him: "Moses was one hundred twenty years old when he died; his sight was unimpaired and his vigor had not abated" (34:7). While we might raise our eyebrows at the claim that he was 120 years old and in good shape, there is no reason to doubt that he lived a long life. What is important for the biblical author is to recognize that old age does not necessarily incapacitate someone from accomplishing remarkable deeds. In fact, the tradition of the "elders" in the Bible, both Old and New

Testaments, testifies to the belief that leadership positions by and large rested on the shoulders of seniors. The reason is likely the traditional identification of age with wisdom. But what is wisdom?

The Book of Proverbs proclaims in simple terms: "The fear of the LORD is the beginning of wisdom; / but fools despise wisdom and instruction" (1:7, my trans.). This adage is repeated multiple times throughout the wisdom literature of the Old Testament. The psalmist, for instance, reinforces it: "The fear of the LORD is the beginning of wisdom; / all those who practice it have a good understanding" (Psalm 111:10). We should remember that the expression "fear of the Lord" does not mean fear and trembling, as in anxiety before a great and terrible lord. Rather it means awe and respect. It is the kind of "fear" that accompanies the realization that one is a creature, not the Creator. It is a humble attitude, both respectful and awestruck at the Lord's greatness compared to our limitations.

The early Christian community is also said to live in "the fear of the Lord" (Acts 9:31). This attitude, as well as the "comfort of the Holy Spirit," helps to give them courage in the face of persecution. For his part, Paul also acknowledges that disciples should live in "fear of the Lord" because one day we will face judgment, and how we live will be part of that judgment (2 Corinthians 5:11-21). He believes he and his companions in ministry have lived in this humble way as apostles, and he does not hesitate to call the Corinthians to the same lifestyle.

There is another, surprising way the elderly sometimes give witness to awesome achievements in their old age. I refer to true acts of heroism.

The Martyrdom of Eleazar

Although we like to tell stories of heroic *young* people, the Bible also shows that the elderly can be admirable models for heroism. One such tale is found in another deuterocanonical book, Second Maccabees (6:18-31). The two books of Maccabees date from the time of the Jewish resistance to foreign domination about 150 years before Christ. It was a difficult period for the Jews because increasing influence from the Greco-Roman world threatened their way of life, their religion, and their very identity. Under the evil Seleucid King Antiochus IV, the Jews were being forced to make sacrifices to foreign gods and to violate their religious laws. One story from the period concerns an old man named Eleazar. It begins thus:

> Eleazar, one of the scribes in high position, a man now advanced in age and of noble presence, was being forced to open his mouth to eat swine's flesh. But he, welcoming death with honor rather than life with pollution, went up to the rack of his own accord, spitting out the flesh. (2 Maccabees 6:18-19)

As the story continues, we learn that Eleazar is ninety years old and yet he is threatened with torture and death if he does not accede to eating pork in violation of the Jewish prohibition against doing so. Even some of his persecutors try to convince him only to pretend to eat the unlawful meat, counting on the likelihood that he would be treated more kindly because of his age. Eleazar's courageous response follows:

> But making a high resolve, worthy of his years and the dignity of his old age and the gray hairs that he had reached with distinction and his excellent life even from childhood, and moreover according to the holy God-given law, he declared himself quickly, telling them to send him to Hades.

> "Such pretense is not worthy of our time of life," he said, "for many of the young might suppose that Eleazar in his ninetieth year had gone over to an alien religion, and through my pretense, for the sake of living a brief moment longer, they would be led astray because of me, while I defile and disgrace my old age. Even if for the present I would avoid the punishment of mortals, yet whether I live or die I shall not escape the hands of the Almighty. Therefore, by bravely giving up my life now, I will show myself worthy of my old age and leave to the young a noble example of how to die a good death willingly and nobly for the revered and holy laws."

When he had said this, he went at once to the rack. (verses 23-28)

The passage ends with Eleazar's horrible death and his testimony that he preferred to die a noble death rather than defy his religious values and his Lord. The text concludes simply: "So in this way he died, leaving in his death an example of nobility and a memorial of courage, not only to the young but to the great body of his nation" (verse 31).

As this story shows, the elderly can sometimes be surprisingly resourceful in their capacity to bear suffering. In their faithfulness to higher values, and despite their frailty and physical weakness, the elderly can in fact bear witness to the ideal of enduring even severe pain for the sake of more important values. Eleazar's temptation was not merely to eat pork, but to violate his religious principles. He showed himself to be a man of integrity.

Lest we think such heroism is restricted to men, the Bible surprises us with a comparable story about an unnamed mother (though she is not said to be elderly) and her seven sons. We do not have space here to recount the whole story; you can read it for yourself in 2 Maccabees chapter 7. It occurs in the same period as that of Eleazar and follows directly after his death. It is basically another tale of unjust persecution. It describes how the mother and her sons are arrested, tortured, and eventually put to death. The king tries to force them to violate their Jewish laws. One by one, he has each son tortured and killed while the others look on. One by one, each son is horribly tortured but refuses to surrender to the king's wishes. Each of them dies a horrific death, but with the encouragement of their mother, who urges them to endure for God's sake, they do not yield to the temptation to deny their faith. At last, the mother herself is tortured and killed: one more heroic act on the part of someone of mature years.

What I believe these stories from the Bible show us is that growing old itself need not prevent us from acting in accordance with our integrity and courage. How we live, and how we die, are more important than simply existing. The heroic tales of the elderly, which go far beyond the Bible, give testimony to this.

Acceptance of Aging

Another aspect worth pursuing briefly is the issue of how well people accept growing older. I know people who view each coming birthday with great trepidation. While it is true that many very elderly people die close to a birthday (I have personally seen this numerous times), the fear of advancing years can seem exaggerated. I once knew a person who, within days of her birthday, would shut herself up in the house, refuse to see people, resist any attempt to celebrate her birthday, and basically go into hiding until it was over. I once gingerly posed the question of "why." Her response was not terribly surprising. She viewed every birthday (after about age thirty!) as one more step toward approaching death. She liked to think of herself as a "young woman." To some degree, she was, even as she aged. But her excessive fear of aging marred her otherwise upbeat spirit, and this baffled her friends who otherwise were very supportive.

I have known others who have shown nothing but grace as they age. They are not naïve. They know that aging means death is drawing nearer. But there is no real anxiety. They appear to take life for what it is. They have arrived at a stage where age has brought with it certain challenges. If they could, they would prefer not to face them, yet they accept them.

In the Bible, there is at least one story of graciousness in old age. The tale of Barzillai the Gileadite illustrates beautifully both some of the tenderness of old age and its frailties. The text describes Barzillai as "a very aged man, eighty years old" (2 Samuel 19:32). Being wealthy, he had been kind to King David, offering him food when he needed it. David naturally wanted to repay the kindness and invited Barzillai to accompany him to the palace in Jerusalem. Barzillai's poignant response reveals his recognition of his own frailty.

> But Barzillai said to the king, "How many years have I still to live, that I should go up with the king to Jerusalem? Today I am eighty years old; can I discern what is pleasant and what is not? Can your servant taste what he eats or what he drinks? Can I still listen to the voice of singing men and singing women? Why then should your servant

be an added burden to my lord the king? Your servant will go a little way over the Jordan with the king. Why should the king recompense me with such a reward? Please let your servant return, so that I may die in my own town, near the graves of my father and my mother." (19:34-37)

King David accedes to the old man's wish and allows another servant to accompany him instead. Notice that Barzillai's condition describes many an aged person. He can't taste what he eats or drinks, because taste changes with age. He can no longer appreciate good singers—perhaps because of poor hearing!—and he also sees that his death is not far away. Not knowing how much time he has left, he wants to die with his ancestors.

To conclude this chapter, I simply note that we all have, to some degree, the ability to control our reaction to the natural process of growing older. We may fear it, or we may embrace it. We may become angry about it, or we may try to put it to its best use. What we cannot do is avoid it.

For Reflection:

- How would you describe your personal attitude toward growing older? Have there been particular influences on your life that have helped shape your attitudes?

- Can you think of any modern examples of courage in old age?

Chapter Six

When Old Age Makes Life Unbearable

There is another aspect of old age that we cannot ignore—the temptations that sometimes accompany the inevitable decline we described in the previous chapter. I can recall the almost innumerable times that old people asked me during our conversations, "Why doesn't God just take me? Why does he keep me around? I'm falling apart. I'm ready! I'm tired. I want to go home!"

Even as a priest, I have a difficult time responding to such questions. I am loathe to give the simplistic response I have sometimes heard among chaplains in nursing homes: "God has a plan for you. You're still useful in God's eyes. You need to be courageous." While there is truth in such responses, they really do not match the depth of feeling or the sentiment of growing discouragement in the wake of the mounting troubles of old age. This is truer for those whose mental faculties have not declined as much as their physical ones. Having once worked in a nursing home as a physical therapy assistant and an orderly, I can say firsthand that many of the elderly I encountered there essentially suffered from depression. As they saw their life ebbing away in little increments, they became more and more discouraged. This was compounded especially if they had no family or friends to visit them, or when these did not go out of their way to be present to them.

Given the many physical and mental challenges that the elderly face in our modern, technologically advanced societies, some people have decided that they cannot bear the thought of growing old in a way that will incapacitate them. While the quality of one's life is clearly an important consideration, I think one of the most dangerous trends in the modern world is the bland acceptance of affirming one's right to choose death whenever one wants. This is not a pretty picture, but we should examine it to see if any direction can be gleaned from the Bible.

I begin with a moving experience I had while viewing a French film that directly tackled the question of choosing to end one's life in the face of a terrible decline in health. Titled *Amour* (French for "love"), the film by famed Austrian director Michael Haneke won the main competition at the Cannes Film Festival in 2012. It tells a simple story of two teachers of classical music who, in their retirement and old age, remain very much in love. When a sudden and unexpected stroke incapacitates the wife, we see the husband selflessly care for her in the most tender of ways. Their daughter returns to Paris from London, where she lives with her husband, to find her previously dynamic and vibrant mother almost totally helpless. She is paralyzed, her speech is slurred, and she cannot do even the most basic human tasks without help. As the movie develops we see the couple come face-to-face with a terrible decision: can they accept her debilitation and maintain their dignity, or will they decide simply to end their lives while they can?

The movie is very well done, with gorgeous music and a realistic portrait of the countless number of couples who find themselves in similar life-threatening situations. I will not reveal the ending, but I will say that the film does not over-sentimentalize the situation. It is an honest attempt by a cinematographer to portray one of the most difficult moral dilemmas of our day: euthanasia.

The Specter of Euthanasia

One of the realities facing modern life is the increasing demand for people to take control of their own lives and determine when they want to end them. In a culture that defines individual, personal rights as *the* most important value, this is a huge temptation. Several countries around the world have already passed laws permitting euthanasia, which is the willful termination of one's own life "on demand." Euthanasia (from Greek *euthanatos*, "easy death") is defined as "the act or practice of killing or permitting the death of hopelessly sick or injured individuals . . . in a relatively painless way for reasons of mercy." The verb form is "euthanize."[7]

There are several different forms of euthanasia. Voluntary euthanasia is when someone desires to end their life, usually to escape excessive pain and suffering. Involuntary euthanasia, which acts against the will of the patient, is essentially murder. Non-voluntary euthanasia occurs when the consent of the victim cannot be obtained, perhaps because they are totally unconscious. In addition, euthanasia can be described as active or passive. Whereas active euthanasia is when someone takes steps to end his or her life by accepting lethal drugs or massive doses of painkillers, passive euthanasia entails withholding substances necessary for life, such as food and water, until the person dies.

It does not take a genius to recognize that this topic is fraught with all kinds of ethical complexity. It is also highly emotional, especially when it comes to the elderly. Some famous people have expressed the desire to end their life because of unbearable pain or the inability to tolerate growing older. They insist that they want to choose when and how they die. They equally insist that it is their right. Thus they opt for euthanasia. There are even countries where one can go for "euthanasia tourism." People are welcome to come and die there!

At present, euthanasia in one form or another is legal in the following countries: Netherlands, Belgium, Canada, Luxembourg, and Colombia. In the USA, the following states permit euthanasia or assisted suicide: Washington, Oregon, Colorado, Hawaii, Vermont, Montana, Washington, D.C., and California. It is remarkable to see how seductive the temptation to approve euthanasia is.

This book is not about moral theology. Our goal is not to explore in detail why the Catholic Church, among other religious institutions, opposes euthanasia on ethical grounds. Rather, we want to put it in the perspective of the process of aging. In reality, when euthanasia has been practiced in the past, such as by the Nazis during World War II, it was not merely the elderly or infirm who were targeted for extermination. They also euthanized Jews simply because of their ethnic/religious identity, the mentally and physically handicapped, homosexuals, "degenerate" artists, Catholic priests, and others who were deemed a burden or threat to society.

A major problem with euthanasia is that it usurps the power of life and death from God and places it in human hands. But in our hands, it becomes a slippery slope. Who determines when it is right to end one's life? Who decides when one becomes too old to be of use to humanity? We risk playing God, when we are merely creatures with both limited lifespans and limited capacity to understand the mysteries of life and death. One can understand the elderly who plead that they are tired of living. One can also understand the terrible anguish of having to endure severe pain. But we should remember that while the Church absolutely opposes euthanasia, it recognizes that modern medicine rightfully can and should use all available morally acceptable means to alleviate pain and suffering to the highest degree possible.

I clearly remember watching someone in his nineties who was suffering from severe breathing difficulties. He had been a lifelong smoker and was suffering from lung cancer and emphysema. As his illness progressed, his breathing became more labored. Not only was oxygen constantly needed, but he also had to be given higher and higher doses of morphine just to allow him a minimum of comfort. As his body weakened and the painkiller took effect over time, he ultimately drifted off, quietly dying in peace. This was not euthanasia. He was not actively pursuing death, nor were his doctors. Rather, they did what they could to alleviate the terrible suffering he endured and to prepare him for the inevitable. They tried to keep him comfortable in his final days.

It is useful here to cite the *Catechism of the Catholic Church* with regard to euthanasia.[8] Its teaching is succinct and clear. Although this particular teaching does not concern the elderly specifically, they can be seen within its scope. On the one hand, it affirms the dignity of all who find themselves in a diminished state. "Those whose lives are diminished or weakened deserve special respect. Sick or handicapped persons should be helped to lead lives as normal as possible" (*CCC*, 2276). On the other hand, the *Catechism* acknowledges the desire of some to take life and death into their own hands and to invoke the good intentions of euthanasia. It condemns such a perspective. "Whatever its motives and means, direct euthanasia consists in putting an end to the lives of handicapped, sick, or dying persons. It is morally unacceptable" (2277). Finally, the *Catechism* recognizes the value of palliative care, that is, ways to reduce someone's suffering as death advances.

> The use of painkillers to alleviate the sufferings of the dying, even at the risk of shortening their days, can be morally in conformity with human

dignity if death is not willed either as an end or a means, but only foreseen and tolerated as inevitable. Palliative care is a special form of disinterested charity. As such it should be encouraged. (2279)

We should notice in these citations that the Bible is not used as a support for this teaching. The Bible does not really offer explicit teaching in this regard. Yet the basic orientation of the entire teaching of the Bible to the sacred origins of human life and its inherent dignity justifies taking the moral stance against euthanasia that is evident in the *Catechism*'s teaching.

While I sympathize with elderly persons who see no hope in their life and perhaps wish to end it, there is nothing in the biblical teaching that would permit euthanasia. On the contrary, the Bible uniformly promotes that God is both the author and source of life. God alone should determine our fate. To explore this aspect a bit more, we need to raise the issue of suicide.

Contemplating Suicide

The Bible, perhaps surprisingly, does not *explicitly* prohibit suicide, the taking of one's own life. The fifth commandment is "You shall not kill" (Exodus 20:13, NABRE). Maybe one could legitimately interpret its meaning as "You shall not *murder*" (NRSV), which would also prohibit killing oneself (but not killing in self-defense, by accident, or in war, for example). But we should also remember that the Bible recognizes that there are instances when offering up one's own life is acceptable, such as when Jesus proclaims:

> For this reason the Father loves me, because I lay down my life in order to take it up again. No one takes it from me, but I lay it down of my own accord. I have power to lay it down, and I have power to take it up again. I have received this command from my Father. (John 10:17-18)

He puts these words into action by his suffering and death on the cross. But this action, in fulfillment of his Father's will, is undertaken for the sake of others, not to avoid some sort of suffering, pain, or terrible experience. On the contrary, it is embracing pain and suffering for the sake of a higher value. It is not considered suicide but a voluntary self-sacrifice on behalf of others. It is how Jesus most concretely shows himself to be the Good Shepherd. Poetically, Jesus explains this attitude with a metaphor: "Very truly, I tell you, unless a grain of wheat falls into the earth and dies, it remains just a single grain; but if it dies, it bears much fruit" (John 12:24). Offering oneself up for the sake of others paradoxically bears new life, not death.

Beyond the unique story of Jesus of Nazareth, there are several stories about actual suicides in the Bible, most of them from the Old Testament. The most famous is that of King Saul. At the end of his reign as the first king of Israel, Saul was losing the battle against the Philistines who were pursuing him bitterly. They killed his sons and mortally wounded Saul himself. In light of his desperate situation, Saul decides to take his own life. The text describes the situation thus:

> The Philistines overtook Saul and his sons; and the Philistines killed Jonathan and Abinadab and Malchishua, the sons of Saul. The battle pressed hard upon Saul; the archers found him, and he was badly wounded by them. Then Saul said to his armor-bearer, "Draw your sword and thrust me through with it, so that these uncircumcised may not come and thrust me through, and make sport of me." But his armor-bearer was unwilling; for he was terrified. So Saul took his own sword and fell upon it. When his armor-bearer saw that Saul was dead, he also fell upon his sword and died with him. So Saul and his three sons and his armor-bearer and all his men died together on the same day. (1 Samuel 31:2-6)

Note that Saul's suicide is to escape capture and humiliation by the enemy, while his armor-bearer kills himself apparently out of devotion to his king.

A similar example in the context of battle is found in the figure of Abimelech, who became king of Israel through treachery. The Bible notes his fate as a suicide, after a woman drops a huge stone on his head, mortally wounding him.

> Immediately he called to the young man who carried his armor and said to him, "Draw your

sword and kill me, so people will not say about me, 'A woman killed him.'" So the young man thrust him through, and he died. (Judges 9:54)

Abimelech seeks to escape the humiliation of having been fatally wounded by a woman!

A third example is Ahithophel. He was a one-time advisor to King David who then decided to desert him in order to follow David's son Absalom, who rebelled against his father and tried to usurp the kingdom. At one point, however, Absalom refuses to follow Ahithophel's advice, and the following is the result:

When Ahithophel saw that his counsel was not followed, he saddled his donkey and went off home to his own city. He set his house in order, and hanged himself; he died and was buried in the tomb of his father. (2 Samuel 17:23)

The fourth example is quite famous: the powerful leader Samson, who was betrayed into the hands of the Philistines by Delilah (Judges 16:4-31). The Philistines blind Samson and then call him out of prison into the temple of their pagan god Dagon in order to make sport of him. He is tied between two columns. Instead of submitting to his humiliation Samson cries out to God and pulls the columns down, causing the entire temple to collapse, killing almost everyone inside, including Samson himself. But in this instance, as with Eleazar, the Judeo-Christian tradition has not really considered it suicide but martyrdom, a self-sacrifice for a greater cause.

A fifth example comes from the New Testament and is equally well known: Judas Iscariot, the traitor. Two different biblical stories narrate his suicide. One is the tradition of Matthew's Gospel, in which having finally recognized his treachery against Jesus of Nazareth, Judas returns the thirty pieces of silver he was paid to betray Jesus to the Jewish leaders and goes out and hangs himself (Matthew 27:3-10). The Acts of the Apostles tells a different story, claiming, "Now [Judas Iscariot] acquired a field with the reward of his wickedness; and falling headlong, he burst open in the middle and all his bowels gushed out" (Acts 1:18). In both instances, the biblical authors see Judas's suicide as the natural consequence of his evil deed in betraying Jesus. Both also associate his death with the establishment of a cemetery for foreigners called "the Field of Blood" (Matthew 27:8; Acts 1:19). Both also see his suicide as a fulfillment of Scripture in which such an evil deed does not go unpunished.

There is also one example in the Bible of someone who seems to have *contemplated* suicide but never acted on it. This is the figure of Job. He is the main example of an innocent victim of suffering, which the Book of Job sees as a special trial to confirm Job's faith in God. You will remember that Job goes so far as to curse the day of his birth, but not to curse God. In his complaint to God, Job cries out:

> "You scare me with dreams / and terrify me with visions, / so that I would choose strangling / and death rather than this body. / I loathe my life; I

would not live forever. / Let me alone, for my days are a breath. / What are human beings, that you make so much of them, / that you set your mind on them, / visit them every morning, / test them every moment?" (7:14-18, see also 13:14-15)

Elsewhere, Job questions why he was even allowed to live.

"Why did I not die at birth, / come forth from the womb and expire? / Why were there knees to receive me, / or breasts for me to suck? / Now I would be lying down and quiet; / I would be asleep; then I would be at rest. . . . / Or why was I not buried like a stillborn child, / like an infant that never sees the light?" (3:11-16)

In Job, perhaps, we get a glimpse of the apparent emptiness and hopelessness of life that sometimes leads people to contemplate suicide. In fact, in modern times, even the Catholic Church has come to recognize that those who actually commit suicide are usually in such a tortured and complex psychological state that they are perhaps not to be condemned. If in ages past the Church refused burial rights to such persons, that is no longer the case. We usually cannot know the deep reasons in a person's life that would lead them to take such a drastic, irreversible action as suicide. While the Church does not accept suicide as a proper response to suffering, it recognizes that an individual's state of mind might be clouded in taking such a dramatic action. The *Catechism of the Catholic Church* succinctly states this teaching:

> We should not despair of the eternal salvation of persons who have taken their own lives. By ways known to him alone, God can provide the opportunity for salutary repentance. The Church prays for persons who have taken their own lives. (2283)

We should also note that among the early Christians, some began to be drawn to the idea of martyrdom in order to imitate Jesus in accepting his fate. If Jesus did it, why shouldn't we? This attitude became such a problem that it led to individuals seeking martyrdom too easily, seeing it as a quick path to sainthood. Saints like Clement of Alexandria (second century AD) had to preach against such a temptation as a false path. Voluntarily seeking martyrdom came to be seen as tantamount to suicide. It was St. Augustine in the fourth century AD who made the distinction between martyrdom and suicide. The former was permissible when it happened by virtue of defending the faith under persecution. The latter was unacceptable because it acts contrary to God's promotion of human life. To this day, most Christians see suicide as a desperate act to be avoided. The sufferings of old age do not permit suicide. While we cannot harshly judge one's motivations or state of mind in such cases, we likewise should not encourage or sanction it. The biblical tradition, then, provides no justification for either euthanasia or suicide.

Once more it is useful to quote from the *Catechism of the Catholic Church.* Its teaching on suicide follows directly upon that concerning euthanasia.[9] In this case, it directly connects the biblical teaching against killing (or murder) with the Church's opposition to suicide. "Suicide is seriously contrary to justice, hope, and charity. It is forbidden by the fifth commandment" (2325).

Sadly, you may be aware of numerous stories of murder-suicide, especially in certain cases where the suffering of an elderly spouse has led to their partner taking dramatic action. The defense of such incidents is usually described as "mercy killing." But it only compounds the ethical complexity of the situation. It is not morally right. Our modern tendency to exalt personal individual rights over those of the wider human community will unfortunately likely push people in the direction of seeing euthanasia, a form of suicide, as a valid choice in the face of wasting away in old age. That would be most unfortunate, and in my opinion, not morally acceptable. Old age has much more to offer than burdens.

For Reflection:

- How do you view the "unbearable suffering" of some people in old age? How do you think it should be addressed? Are there ethical considerations that should be taken into account?

- Why is human life itself not always an absolute value? That is, under what circumstances might it be acceptable to give one's own life (not take another person's) for a greater value?

Chapter Seven

Intergenerational Conflict: When the Boomers Meet the Millennials

Sociologists teach us that each succeeding generation has certain characteristics that define it. I happen to be part of the generation called the "baby boomers." These are people who were born just after World War II (from 1945 to 1964). We are so numerous and are living such long lives that we are impacting many issues concerning retirement. The title derives from the fact that just after World War II, more babies were born in 1946 than ever before. That was the "boom." The trend continued until the decline in the mid-1960s. By then, boomers made up about 40 percent of the US population.

Other generations who have come after the boomers include "generation X" or "gen X" (born from about 1965-1976), "generation Y" or "millennials" (born from about 1977-1996), and most recently "generation Z" (born from about 1996 to the mid-2000s). These are artificial and fluid designations, of course. Sociologists differ on precise definitions, timelines, and characteristics of each generation. Each group tends to have its own music, its own self-description, and so on. What is clear, though, is that as people age, there is the possibility of being more and more removed from succeeding generations. It becomes harder to understand one another. What develops is called a "generation gap." It can also lead to intergenerational conflict.

For me, one of the clear signs of the "generation gap" of my era concerned trends in style and music in the 1960s. My parents generally objected to long hair, beards, rock music, and of course, drugs and alcohol. ("Free sex," symbolized by the musical *Hair* in 1968 and the Woodstock Music Festival phenomenon in 1969, did not even remotely enter my parents' vocabulary.) Maybe "objected" is too strong a word. They barely tolerated it to some degree, but everyone knew that they did not favor such "modern" trends.

Another example of generational differences became apparent to me as a young priest. I used to preach occasional youth retreats, and one of the exercises on the retreat was to read Gospel parables. I invited the young teenagers, gathered in small groups, to choose a parable, which they would then study and act out in some form for all the groups. On one occasion, a group chose the beloved story of the Good Samaritan (Luke 10:29-37). When they acted out the story, it was given a modern setting. Their version went something like this.

Once there was a teenager on his way to basketball practice when he was set upon by a group of motorcycle grandmothers. They stripped him, beat him, and left him by the side of road, and took off with all his possessions. A teacher came by, noticed the poor victim, and bypassed him. Then a priest came by, saw the wounded boy, and ignored him. Finally, an obviously effeminate young man (played in an exaggerated and humorous way) came on the scene, and was the only one to see that he was taken to an emergency room and properly cared for.

The reaction of the others was hilarious. It was so well acted out, and somehow it "hit the mark" with the young audience. But it was also faithful to the Gospel story. What struck me later, in conversation with a woman who was one of the chaperones, were the images that the kids had used. She pointed out to me that speaking of "motorcycle grandmothers," for example, hinted at the generational differences that kids often feel. They do not find it easy to identify with their grandparents' viewpoints, and vice versa, especially moving into adolescence. Also, the chaperone pointed out that the image of the effeminate hero of the story pointed to the underlying struggle adolescents go through to find their true sexual identity. The fact that the story was told at a time when homosexuality was being more and more discussed in the open was also likely a factor. Overall, I was struck that the exercise seemed to have provoked some profound thought on the part of the retreatants, who also enjoyed the experience.

Biblical Perspectives

Does the Bible indicate any sensitivity to this generational conflict? While it is not a major theme in the Bible, there is some evidence of generational differences. One example occurs in First Samuel. Eli the priest's sons are called "scoundrels," and in his old age, he seems to have lost influence over them (2:12-17,22-23). The story shows the sad conflict between arrogant youths and their father.

Another example is found in the curious story of the prophet Elisha on his way to the shrine at Bethel.

> He went up from there to Bethel; and while he was going up on the way, some small boys came out of the city and jeered at him, saying, "Go away, baldhead! Go away, baldhead!" When he turned around and saw them, he cursed them in the name of the LORD. Then two she-bears came out of the woods and mauled forty-two of the boys. From there he went on to Mount Carmel, and then returned to Samaria. (2 Kings 2:23-25)

This story might well be classified as dark humor from the Bible. Since forty-two of the boys are mauled by the two bears, we can see that the gang of youngsters who are mocking the prophet because of his baldness—and thus his age—must have been large indeed. Note also that they are called "small boys," emphasizing the age gap between them and the prophet. But the fact that Elisha "curses" them—and old people can be good at cursing—and then the two bears miraculously come out of the woods and attack them, seems to show that God does not tolerate mocking people in their old age. There are consequences to be paid for such mockery.

It is true that young people sometimes mock the elderly because of their physical characteristics. As we age, we tend to lose our hair or have it turn gray or snow-white. We also gain weight, or perhaps lose it, noticeably. We walk with less sure steps, we have trouble maintaining our balance, and we are perhaps bent over. But age is not merely a matter of physical characteristics, but of character and of mental substance. Whatever the original meaning of the text, it does show that intergenerational conflict did not begin in modern times. It is likely something that has been rooted in human experience since time immemorial.

A late prophetic book of the Old Testament provides some evidence that inter-generational harmony was the ideal to be maintained. God promises that a time will come in which such will be the standard.

> Lo, I will send you the prophet Elijah before the great and terrible day of the LORD comes. He will turn the hearts of parents to their children and the hearts of children to their parents, so that I will not come and strike the land with a curse. (Malachi 4:5-6)

The background of this text is the promise of the return of Elijah, Elisha's mentor, who had miraculously been taken up to heaven in a fiery chariot (2 Kings 2:11). He was to return one day as the forerunner of the messiah. The New Testament sees in this figure John the Baptist, who came as the forerunner of Jesus the Messiah (Matthew 11:14). Indeed, the ideal vision of Jesus in much of his teaching is that in the kingdom of God, all will be one. There will be harmony and concord. Divisions, including those between young and old, will cease (Galatians 3:28).

The prophet Zechariah expresses a similar view of the harmony between generations when the messianic age dawns: "Old men and old women shall again sit in the streets of Jerusalem, each with staff in hand because of their great age. And the streets of the city shall be full of boys and girls playing in its streets" (8:4-5).

Exploitation of the Elderly

One of the clear dangers for the elderly in our day is the possibility that they can be exploited. Their senses and their reflexes are not as keen as they once were, and thus they sometimes can be manipulated or taken advantage of in unfair ways. This happens occasionally over the telephone, when people claiming to be from the IRS or some government agency call to demand payment of back taxes or some bogus penalty. They coerce the elderly into revealing their bank account information, making them vulnerable to fraud. Seniors can also be exploited by their own dishonest children or grandchildren, who try to gain access to their wealth illegitimately. There have been countless incidents of family fraud and wrangling over estates of elderly relatives. It seems there is no end to schemes to defraud older citizens, which is why there are now government programs to alert senior citizens to possible fraud.

Even more despicable is the treatment the elderly sometimes receive in the very homes designed to care for them. Some are left unattended for hours on end, slumped over in wheelchairs and ignored. Still others are poorly treated when they soil themselves; poorly paid staff resent having to clean up the mess, wrongly blaming the patient for what cannot be helped. Sadly, exploitation of the elderly is a modern reality in multiple countries.

One finds such unfortunate tales even in the Bible. Two examples suffice, both found in the Book of Genesis. The first concerns Noah, and the second concerns Lot.

Noah's story is simple enough. After having ridden out the great flood in the ark and having accepted God's generous offer of a covenant, with the sign of the rainbow, Noah now must set about repopulating the earth. In a sense, Noah is the beginning of a "new creation."

> The sons of Noah who went out of the ark were Shem, Ham, and Japheth. Ham was the father of Canaan. These three were the sons of Noah; and from these the whole earth was peopled. Noah, a man of the soil, was the first to plant a vineyard. He drank some of the wine and became drunk, and he lay uncovered in his tent. And Ham, the father of Canaan, saw the nakedness of his father, and told his two brothers outside. Then Shem and Japheth took a garment, laid it on both their shoulders, and walked backward and covered the

nakedness of their father; their faces were turned away, and they did not see their father's nakedness. When Noah awoke from his wine and knew what his youngest son had done to him, he said, "Cursed be Canaan; / lowest of slaves shall he be to his brothers." (Genesis 9:18-25)

In this story, Noah's youngest son Ham seriously embarrasses his father, who has gotten drunk on wine, by apparently making fun of his father's accidental nakedness. He tells his older brothers (as a joke?) who respectfully cover their father's nudity with a garment. They are careful not to look upon their father's naked state. What we must remember here is that, in comparison to other ancient peoples, the Jews had a particular aversion to nudity, especially because of its association with defeat. In war, the victor led the defeated armies away naked in shame. In the Noah story, the younger son Ham, who is the father of Canaan, shames his father and becomes the symbol of the later shameful religious practices of the Canaanites. This, in fact, is the purpose of the story: to show the origins of the shameful pagan practices associated with nudity and sexuality that the Israelites would later despise. But it is also a case of a young man placing an elderly father in a position to be mocked.

Another part of the background is Israel's culture of honor and shame. In the biblical world, much more so than in our own, life was lived according to the values of honor and shame. Whatever brought honor to the family, the tribe, or the nation was deeply desirable. In contrast, whatever brought shame to these entities by some individual's disgusting actions could barely be lived down. Shame lingered and tainted the entire community, not simply the individual. In such a culture, the actions of Noah's children would have been a serious violation of propriety.

Lot's story is a bit more disgusting, especially from our modern viewpoint. It concerns incest, which even the ancients found repulsive. The biblical text lays out the story explicitly.

> Now Lot went up out of Zoar and settled in the hills with his two daughters, for he was afraid to stay in Zoar; so he lived in a cave with his two daughters. And the firstborn said to the younger, "Our father is old, and there is not a man on earth to come in to us after the manner of all the world. Come, let us make our father drink wine, and we will lie with him, so that we may preserve offspring through our father." So they made their father drink wine that night; and the firstborn went in, and lay with her father; he did not know when she lay down or when she rose. On the next day, the firstborn said to the younger, "Look, I lay last night with my father; let us make him drink wine tonight also; then you go in and lie with him, so that we may preserve offspring through our father." So they made their father drink wine that night also; and the

younger rose, and lay with him; and he did not know when she lay down or when she rose. Thus both the daughters of Lot became pregnant by their father. (Genesis19:30-36)

By any measure, this is not the way to treat your "old man." The Bible does not shy away from human problems. This one is particularly offensive, although there are some special circumstances. The whole story takes place in the context of God's destruction of the notorious cities of Sodom and Gomorrah. One circumstance is that Lot flees to Zoar to escape the Lord's destruction of the two cities whose citizens are wicked; for example, the men of the city wanted to have sex with the two angels who had come to Lot's house in the form of men. Lot offered the citizens his daughters (no way to treat your children, either!) instead. In the end, Lot, his wife, and their two daughters leave the area to escape the coming wrath. That is when they find themselves in the middle of nowhere.

A second factor might also be somewhat understandable. The two young women worry that they won't be able to find husbands—a crucial need if they were to survive. So they wickedly contrive to get their father drunk and, one after the other, have sex with him. The resulting sons are named Moab and Ammon, thus representing tribes that eventually become enemies of Israel.

Taken together, the circumstances surrounding the daughters' incest with their elderly father do not justify their actions. Yet they happened. The story of Lot shows how easily one can manipulate the elderly for one's own designs, especially with the aid of alcohol. Unfortunately, we know that such instances of "elder abuse" still happen, both within family structures and also by outsiders who simply look for vulnerable prey.

There is possibly a counter-story in the Bible concerning a young person acting favorably toward an elder. In the Acts of the Apostles, St. Paul's unnamed nephew (described as a "young man," Greek *neanias*) warns the authorities of a plot against his uncle's life (Acts 23:16-22). While this may be more the case of acting on behalf of a family member, it also shows the courage of a young man acting decisively to protect an older man.

Modern Perspectives

One of the attempts to overcome intergenerational differences can be seen in the way Pope St. John Paul II and his successors have used World Youth Day to draw attention to young people as the hope of the future. It was indeed quite remarkable to see the appeal John Paul II had for young people, especially on those grand occasions when hundreds of thousands of youth would come to hear him evangelize. As he grew increasingly old and debilitated from his advanced Parkinson's disease, he never ceased to interact with the young in an effective way. Those around would observe how his eyes would light up when he gazed upon the groups of youths who often shouted out slogans like, "John Paul II, we love you!" True, this pope had a particularly outgoing personality and was a true actor. He did, after all, have a background in theatre. But the interaction between him and the crowds of young people was not merely a show. There was genuine "electricity" there that captivated his young audience. This is still what is needed today, as the world's population grows increasingly older while at the same time hordes of youth continue to come on the scene and look to embrace a future that is more theirs than ours.

Pope Francis has his own appeal among the young, which has also been apparent during the World Youth Days that he attended. He once made an explicit plea for the young generation to cherish their grandparents. In a tweet in July 2018, he said: "Grandparents are a treasure in the family. Please, take care of your grandparents: love them and let them talk to your children!"[10] It is not the only time he has encouraged younger folks to respect and take time for their elderly relatives. He has also asked senior citizens to listen to and appreciate what younger generations have to offer. They are, after all, the future. Yet the key is in appreciation of both ends of the human spectrum.

In an important text on the eve of the third Christian millennium, one of the Roman agencies charged with oversight of lay people enunciated the importance of both generations:

> Older people represent the "historical memory" of the younger generations. They are the bear-

ers of fundamental human values. Where this memory is lacking, people are rootless; they also lack any capacity to project themselves with hope towards a future that transcends the limits of the present.[11]

We need one another. All the more reason why intergenerational gaps should be resisted, and open conversations between generations fostered.

For Reflection:

- Have you personally experienced a generation gap? Among acquaintances? In your family? How do you approach such a situation?

- What methods might be used to bring young people and old people more in tune with one another? Is intergenerational conflict inevitable or avoidable?

Chapter Eight

Life after Living:
Memory and Generativity in Old Age

As a boomer, I am part of a generation that is slowly (or quickly?) passing away. As we boomers age, one of the things we have encountered, and which accompanies most older people, is a loss of memory. Have you been frustrated when you can't remember where you placed your keys? Your cell phone? Your calendar or address book?

One of my worst memories (ironically) about loss of memory is when I had parked my car at an airport parking lot for a short trip of two days. Upon my return, I was absolutely sure that I had parked the car on a certain level in the parking lot. I was totally convinced that my memory was correct. Absentmindedly, I had left the parking ticket in the car itself and, though I had made a mental note of the level, color, and sector of the lot I was in, my memory let me down. I walked around for a good hour, going place to place, trying to find the car. I would click my car door opener to see if a car would beep and the lights blink, to no avail. Eventually, a security guard came to my aid. He drove me around until I found my car—not only on a different level, but in a totally different (but similar-looking) lot!

Living Memory

Memory. It is so essential, but we know that as we age, it can dwindle. I have been amazed how frequently the elderly remember events or people from decades ago, but they have trouble remembering what they ate for breakfast, or even if they ate at all. This is a natural phenomenon, even if it strikes people in truly individualistic ways. What is ironic, perhaps, is that old people symbolize the importance of collective memory, just at the time in their life when their own personal memory may be fading.

Remembrance is another word to evoke memory. It has a particular biblical resonance worth recalling as we begin this chapter. The noun "remembrance" and the verb "remember" occur hundreds of times in the Bible. The Hebrew concept (from the root *zakar*, "remember") is vitally important. It is tied especially to God's remembrance of the covenant (Genesis 9:15; Ezekiel 16:60). Although both the noun and the verb are used, it is the verbal idea of remembering that gets the lion's share of attention. To remember is an *active* reality, not a passive one. God remembers the terms of the covenant even when the other party (Israel) forgets. God remembers the promise of mercy, even when the chosen people forget (Jeremiah 31:20).

Memory also functions in the midst of the people. Thus, the good deeds of the Lord are always to be remembered (Exodus 13:3; Psalm 143:5), and important figures from the past are called to mind on a regular basis as well.

They serve as good models, to emulate (Sirach 41:3, 45:1; 2 Maccabees 7:20), or bad models, to shun (Sirach 10:17, 23:26, 44:9).

From a New Testament perspective, the most important connection with remembering is the Eucharist, the celebration of the Lord's Supper (1 Corinthians 11:20). On that occasion, Jesus invited his closest followers: "Do this in remembrance of me" (Luke 22:19; see also 1 Corinthians 11:25). Every time we celebrate the Eucharist, it is in remembrance of the Lord Jesus. Our collective memory is what counts. This is not just about our individual memories, which might in fact become frail or untrustworthy. We are invited to participate rather in a collective memory.

I take this biblical perspective seriously. It touches the experience of the community with regard to older people. Collectively, the Bible exhibits a fondness for the elderly precisely because they constitute a pathway to direct remembrance of the past. Remembering who we are and where we came from is part of their job. The elderly constitute our ancestors. They are the pioneers who forged a path for us to follow and who have left us the task to pick up where they left off.

Ancestors

A popular trend today is family genealogies. Many people have become attracted to searching their family trees. There is great interest in knowing one's heritage, both in terms of ethnic and genetic identity, and also in terms of knowing more about one's distant relatives. There are even DNA tests now that can trace one's lineage through genetic lines. Many young people are interested in this research likely because they are looking for a clearer identity. This trend is assisted greatly by new technological advances. Computers can store huge amounts of data that can be searched within seconds, and this has fueled even greater interest in tracking down one's ancestors.

The late Pope John Paul II wrote eloquently in his 1999 "Letter to the Elderly" of the struggles of his own increasing frailty. But he also emphasized the value of the elderly in society.

> Elderly people help us to see human affairs with greater wisdom, because life's vicissitudes have brought them knowledge and maturity. They are the guardians of our collective memory, and thus the privileged interpreters of that body of ideals and common values which support and guide life in society. (paragraph 10)

Sometimes, you don't need to go far to find information. Many families have a built-in resource: their parents, grandparents, and great-grandparents. One of the dependable habits of older people is to reminisce. I have regularly enjoyed talking with senior citizens who get into deep conversations recalling experiences they had when they were young, calling to mind people I have never met but who somehow made an impression on them. Many of the stories my own father told of his family and growing up during the Depression were both moving and humorous. There were real characters he knew! And some of them were my relatives.

While seniors can perhaps get bogged down with living in the past by such reminiscences, sometimes they also offer a window into distant ancestors that can help us understand why we are who we are. The Bible, too, exhibits an interest in genealogies. Both Matthew and Luke record genealogies relating to Jesus, but they are not the same. Whereas Matthew's revolves around King David's line of rulers (Matthew 1:1-17), Luke's traces Jesus' heritage all the way back to Adam (Luke 3:23-38). Now there's a family lineage!

Other parts of the Bible show an interest in ancestors through a different means. Ben Sira, for instance, has a lengthy section near the end of his book that recounts the deeds of many of Israel's ancestors (Sirach chapters 44—50). He mentions a host of important persons in Israel's history, many of whom we have named in this book because they were persons of stature, age, and wisdom. He names Enoch, Noah, Abraham, Isaac, Moses, Aaron, Phinehas, Joshua, Caleb, Samuel, David, Solomon, and more. Most of these are the heroes of Israel's story. But he does not shy away from some of the "black sheep" of the family. Thus, Solomon's son Rehoboam and servant Jeroboam are named, but are treated harshly because they led Israel into sin. This long list of ancestors serves to do more than hark back to the "good old days." It is a way for Ben Sira to recognize that what really matters most in life is not the length of it but its quality, as we examined in chapter five. His list leads him to a prayer of thanksgiving for having attained wisdom in his long life. The prayer, in fact, is part of an extended temple liturgy in which he apparently participated. In his remembrance, he invokes especially God's mercy. "Then I remembered your mercy, O Lord, / and your kindness from of old, / for you rescue those who wait for you / and save them from the hand of their enemies" (Sirach 51:8).

In a different vein, the Book of Hebrews also has an extended section of remembrance of the ancestors. The author lists what he calls "so great a cloud of witnesses" (12:1) because when he reminisces about Israel's history and how it led to Jesus, the Son of God, he finds the fine thread of faith that can be traced through the ancestors. Thus, he goes on to praise Abel, Enoch, Noah, Abraham, Isaac, Jacob, and Moses. He laments that he does not have time to recall them all, such as Gideon, Barak, Samson, and others, many of whom suffered terribly for the sake of the faith (11:32). Despite the wonderful testimony of all these witnesses to faith through history, he goes on to point out how Jesus far surpasses them in glory. And with such a great lineage to recall, he encourages his community to be strong in resisting the temptation to be discouraged in their own apparent persecution. He urges them to "lift your drooping hands and strengthen your weak knees" (12:12). In this case, the image is not about the elderly—although it is the ancestors of old who are recalled—but a call to resist discouragement. Have faith, and all will be well.

Generativity in One's Old Age

Generativity may seem like a big word, but everyone can recognize what it means. It refers to the capacity to produce something. The word is usually associated with procreation or begetting children, but in recent decades it has become a popular expression among sociologists, psychologists, and others to describe the desire and capacity of people to want to be productive in their lives. Most people desire to leave some kind of legacy. What will I leave behind in the world by which people will remember me? What kind of accomplishment will I have achieved that will endure?

In the Bible, generativity is at the heart of human identity. Having children was more than just a fulfillment of God's command to "Be fruitful and multiply" (Genesis 1:28), though this duty was taken seriously. In the biblical understanding, God created the human person, male and female, to be productive, literally and otherwise. We human beings were thereby given a share in God's unique capacity to *create*. Of course, whereas God created *ex nihilo* (Latin for "out of nothing"; Genesis 1:1-2), we always need materials of some sort. In the case of begetting children, it requires the male's seed and the female's egg. Both are essential to be joined and transformed into a totally new being, a new life, which nonetheless shares some aspects of both parental genetic codes.

We probably think of human procreation as primarily limited to people who are not so advanced in age. From a medical standpoint, it is dangerous for women to conceive past a certain age; this can endanger their own health and/or the health of their unborn child. People in antiquity probably knew this basic truth, even though they did not have the benefit of modern science. Intriguingly, though, the Bible does not limit procreation to the young! Generativity is found quite widely among the elderly.

In antiquity, the infant mortality rate was incredibly high. Consequently, having many children was a way to ensure that one's family had a chance to survive. Males, in particular, were desirable because they provided protection for the family, the tribe, and ultimately the people as a whole. One of the Psalms expresses this viewpoint eloquently.

> Sons are indeed a heritage from the LORD, /the fruit of the womb a reward. / Like arrows in the hand of a warrior / are the sons of one's youth. / Happy is the man who has / his quiver full of them. / He shall not be put to shame / when he speaks with his enemies in the gate. (Psalm 127:3-5)

Sons are a guarantee that a family can withstand enemies, although this same Psalm insists that it is the Lord who "builds the house" and "guards the city" (verse 1).

In ancient Israel, being childless was considered a curse. Women prayed earnestly to have children. Barrenness was scorned. Marriages that were not fertile, and women who were barren, were generally ridiculed. Obviously the older one got, the less chance one had to expect to bear children.

Even the ancients knew that fertility declined with age. Yet there is a remarkable theme that runs through the Bible that shows that God can act in surprising ways with older people. Generativity need not stop in advanced age. Several examples are readily apparent.

The first example comes from Abram (later called Abraham) and Sarai (later called Sarah). We have already seen that Genesis acknowledges this patriarch and matriarch for their old age. The tale, however, also says explicitly that they were childless. Then God intervenes. In the context of the covenant that God offers Abram, God promises a very great "reward" (Genesis 15:1). Indicating his desire to have children, which would guarantee the survival of his name and his heritage, Abram protests. "O Lord God, what will you give me, for I continue childless, and the heir of my house is Eliezer of Damascus? . . . You have given me no offspring, and so a slave born in my house is to be my heir" (Genesis 15:2-3). We can practically hear the anguish in Abram's voice. How humiliating that his only heir will be a servant instead of one from his own flesh. But God counters the protest:

> "This man shall not be your heir; no one but your very own issue shall be your heir." He brought him outside and said, "Look toward heaven and count the stars, if you are able to count them." Then he said to him, "So shall your descendants be." (15:4-5)

Now you can imagine the reaction of Abram, at least in his interior. Although the text says he accepted God's word, which God goes on to explain in detail, Abram must have been skeptical. For as the next chapter admits: "Now Sarai, Abram's wife, bore him no children" (16:1).

Abram must have been a bit desperate, for then he decides to have sex with Sarai's servant Hagar, with Sarai's encouragement. She freely admits, "You see that the LORD has prevented me from bearing children; go in to my slave-girl; it may be that I shall obtain children by her" (Genesis 16:2). And, lo and behold, a son is born, while Abram is a mere eighty-six-year-old (16:16). We should be careful not to be judgmental about this story. In ancient Israel, the practice of having sexual relations with one's servants would not have been considered inappropriate in all circumstances. The story's main goal, however, is to show that God can enable fruitfulness at any age, when he chooses to bless a faithful servant.

Then the plot thickens. Abram's son Ishmael is not a proper heir. Besides, Sarai suddenly becomes jealous of Hagar's fertility and the way Hagar now views her, and mistreats her slave to the point that Hagar tries to run away. The next important scene is the covenant of circumcision with Abram when he was ninety-nine years old (Genesis chapter 17). This covenant not only requires circumcision of all the males of the household, but also entails a name change. Now Abraham and Sarah have a new relationship with God, but there lingers in the background a question of how the original promise of progeny is going to be fulfilled.

The next scene describes the arrival of three strange visitors to Abraham's tent (Genesis chapter 18). Abraham dutifully offers them the customary hospitality, asking Sarah to make a meal. (Women feeding the men again!) Then a curious thing happens as the story unfolds.

> They said to him, "Where is your wife Sarah?" And he said, "There, in the tent." Then one said, "I will surely return to you in due season, and your wife Sarah shall have a son." And Sarah was listening at the tent entrance behind him. Now Abraham and Sarah were old, advanced in age; it had ceased to be with Sarah after the manner of women. So Sarah laughed to herself, saying, "After I have grown old, and my husband is old, shall I have pleasure?" The LORD said to Abraham, "Why did Sarah laugh, and say, 'Shall I indeed bear a child, now that I am old?' Is anything too wonderful for the LORD? At the set time I will return to you, in due season, and Sarah shall have a son." But Sarah denied, saying, "I did not laugh"; for she was afraid. He said, "Oh yes, you did laugh." (18:9-15)

We know the rest of the story. Sarah indeed becomes pregnant and bears a son, Isaac, whose name is a pun in Hebrew on the word for laughter (Genesis chapter 21). This gives her pause to reflect.

> Abraham was a hundred years old when his son Isaac was born to him. Now Sarah said, "God has

brought laughter for me; everyone who hears will laugh with me." And she said, "Who would ever have said to Abraham that Sarah would nurse children? Yet I have borne him a son in his old age." (21:5-7)

So, here is Abraham at age 100 bearing an heir! Nothing is impossible with God. This miracle was not lost on certain New Testament authors. The author of the Letter to the Hebrews, for instance, speaks of Abraham thus: "By faith he received power of procreation, even though he was too old—and Sarah herself was barren—because he considered him faithful who had promised" (Hebrews 11:11). Even though generativity, in the sense of physically having children, is usually limited by chronological age, the reality is that some conceptions and births defy human explanation. Numerous older couples I have known have been surprised when suddenly a "little bundle of joy" arrives when they least expected it. If it is difficult to be a parent when one is young, it is even more a challenge when one is older! Your energy is not the same to keep up with youngsters.

This theme of generativity in old age recurs in numerous other stories in the Old Testament and into the New. For example, the story of the birth of Samson indicates God's ability to make fertile those who are barren (Judges chapter 13). Although his parents' age is not emphasized in this story, there are many similarities to the story of Isaac. Because he is a child that surprisingly comes from barrenness, Samson will be dedicated to God (verse 7).

The New Testament continues this theme in the story of John the Baptist's conception and birth (Luke 1:5-25). John's parents are named Zechariah, a priest who serves in the Jerusalem temple, and Elizabeth. The text comments starkly: "But they had no children, because Elizabeth was barren, and both were getting on in years" (verse 7). One day, while Zechariah attends to his duties in the temple, an angel appears to him with a surprising message: "Do not be afraid, Zechariah, for your prayer has been heard. Your wife Elizabeth will bear you a son, and you will name him John" (verse 13). All seems well and good until Zechariah responds: "How will I know that this is so? For I am an old man, and my wife is getting on in years" (verse 18). This is understandable, is it not? He knows that conceiving children in old age is unlikely. But his question, which likely hides a forthcoming denial, leads to punishment, which the angel explains: "But now, because you did not believe my words, which will be fulfilled in their time, you will become mute, unable to speak, until the day these things occur" (verse 20). Zechariah becomes mute, but in a short time, his wife Elizabeth becomes pregnant, and she praises God, saying, "This is what the Lord has done for me when he looked favorably on me and took away the disgrace I have endured among my people" (verse 25).

This beautiful story is intertwined, of course, with the parallel story of the virginal conception of Jesus in the humble virgin of Nazareth, Mary. But in that well-known story, there is no hint of overcoming the barrier of age, although in both instances, it is God's power that is working behind the scenes. Later, after his son's birth, when Zechariah acknowledges that his name is to be John—despite the fact that no one in the family bears that name—his mute condition is suddenly healed (Luke 1:57-64). Then filled with the Holy Spirit, he proclaims a hymn that we know as the "Canticle of Zechariah" (1:67-79). It is a beautiful hymn of praise for what God has graciously done in Zechariah's life and in Israel's.

There is, however, another elderly pair who feature in Luke's Gospel. The man is Simeon, whose age is not explicitly given, but who must have been quite elderly. The text calls him "righteous and devout" and describes how God promised that he would "not see death before he had seen the Lord's Messiah" (Luke 2:25-26). This promise is fulfilled when Joseph and Mary bring the baby Jesus to the temple to be circumcised in accordance with Jewish law (2:22-24). The old man rejoices when he holds the child in his arms and gives thanks to God, as did Zechariah, with a hymn, which we know as "Simeon's Canticle" (2:29-32).

The woman in this tale, who provides yet another witness to God's blessing upon the elderly, is Anna. (Luke has a nice tendency to balance stories of men with stories of women.) Her story is briefly told.

> There was also a prophet, Anna the daughter of Phanuel, of the tribe of Asher. She was of a great age, having lived with her husband seven years after her marriage, then as a widow to the age of eighty-four. She never left the temple but

worshiped there with fasting and prayer night and day. At that moment she came, and began to praise God and to speak about the child to all who were looking for the redemption of Jerusalem. (Luke 2:36-38)

So here we have an elderly widow, devoted to her own service in the temple, and privileged at the age of eighty-four to witness great things and testify to them. Age is thus no limit to how one can participate in spreading good news.

Widows

Let me propose another possible type of generativity found in the Bible. It is one that may also have modern parallels. I speak here of widows. (In modern terms, one could also speak of widowers, but that is not really addressed in the Bible.) Widows, many of whom were elderly, apparently had a special role in the early Church. Some of the Pauline letters indicate that there was virtually a bona fide ministry of widows. Of course, a woman could become a widow at a young age, and not all widows remarried. But we find an interesting passage that addresses the question of the age of widows in Paul's First Letter to Timothy. In this letter Paul gives advice to Timothy, as one of his appointed successors, about various ministerial offices in the Church. Here is his advice on widows.

Honor widows who are really widows. If a widow has children or grandchildren, they should first learn their religious duty to their own family and make some repayment to their parents; for this is pleasing in God's sight. The real widow, left alone, has set her hope on God and continues in supplications and prayers night and day; but the widow who lives for pleasure is dead even while she lives. Give these commands as well, so that they may be above reproach. And whoever does not provide for relatives, and especially for family members, has denied the faith and is worse than an unbeliever.

Let a widow be put on the list if she is not less than sixty years old and has been married only once; she must be well attested for her good works, as one who has brought up children, shown hospitality, washed the saints' feet, helped the afflicted, and devoted herself to doing good in every way. But refuse to put younger widows on the list; for when their sensual desires alienate them from Christ, they want to marry, and so they incur condemnation for having violated their first pledge. Besides that, they learn to be idle, gadding about from house to house; and they are not merely idle, but also gossips and busybodies, saying what they should not say. So I would have younger widows marry, bear children, and manage their households, so as to give the adversary no occasion to revile us. (1 Timothy 5:3-14)

A number of features of this quotation are important. First, notice that Paul says widows, if they have children or grandchildren, should first be conscious of their duties to their own families. In other words, familial responsibilities take precedence over church needs. Widows should not seek out special duties if they have more pressing obligations to address.

A second observation concerns age. Paul shows concern that younger widows (under sixty, which we have seen before is considered the age at which one reached authentic senior status in ancient Israel) might be tempted by their sexual desires. We might be put off by Paul's apparent sexist attitude that makes of young widows gossips and busybodies. He is not speaking of all women or widows. But he suspects that certain temptations, especially those concerning sexual attraction, are stronger for a younger widow than for an older one. His concern is that widows who are tempted to act in ways that could tarnish their reputation could hurt the community's reputation as well. Thus he recommends being cautious with regard to young widows in formal roles.

Finally, notice that Paul recognizes widows who have already raised their families and thus know how to serve others. While we cannot be certain of the precise duties of widows in the early Church, it seems that their ministry was focused on communal needs. They primarily tended to the community's charitable deeds. The fact that there was a role for widows shows that their lives could indeed continue and contribute to the good of the community even apart from remarrying.

In short, the Bible affirms that age is no barrier to generativity.

For Reflection:

- How do you interpret God's action toward those in the Bible who are sterile and seen as unproductive? Many married couples do not have children, for one reason or another. In what ways can they be "generative," especially as they grow older?

- In what ways do you believe you can be productive as you grow older? Do you have projects in mind that might help you stay active and engaged? What limits do you foresee for yourself?

Chapter Nine

You're Going to Live Forever

This last chapter is a little shorter, as we come close to the end of our exploration of what the Bible says about old age. You are probably familiar with the adage, "you are what you eat." It's meant to recall that what we put in our mouths on a regular basis is going to affect our bodily health. If you eat a lot of junk food, chances are your body will suffer from it. A healthy diet likely will help sustain a healthy body.

I propose an analogy to this saying. Over time, it seems that we essentially "become what we are," or rather, "what we are made of." Modern medicine has shown that our genetic makeup, which comes from our parents, has a major impact on many (but not necessarily all) aspects of our existence. We may have inherited a tendency to being overweight or underweight, being tall or short, having heart troubles, being susceptible to digestion problems, and so on. The point is that, in addition to our own personal developed habits and various outside cultural influences, much of what we are made of comes from our parents. It's in our genes.

One of the phenomena that seems to go along with aging is the realization of how much our parents have influenced our personal identity. I remember on one occasion being with a friend at a restaurant. At the end of the meal, I noticed that she picked up a few packets of sugar and stuck them in her purse. When I raised an eyebrow, she noticed. I quietly asked why she was doing that (I knew she was not poor). She blushed, obviously embarrassed. Then demurely she put the packets back in their place. Then, like a light bulb going on, she explained. "You know what, I think I am turning into my mother! She used to do that, but I suppose in her case, I could understand it. She grew up during the Depression when sugar was a rationed, precious commodity. She always used to stockpile." As we departed and carried on the conversation, she admitted to me that she felt, as she aged, she was becoming more and more like her mother every day. And it was not always the most admirable qualities that she was imitating!

There is a prophetic proverb that is pertinent here. It concerns the consequences of the actions of one's parents on succeeding generations. Both Jeremiah and Ezekiel record the saying in their respective prophetic books. "The parents have eaten sour grapes, / and the children's teeth are set on edge" (Jeremiah 31:29; Ezekiel 18:2). Succeeding generations often pay the price for the sins of their parents and grandparents. Perhaps it is simply the way of the world. But Jesus promised that there was another world to come, in which all that was intended to happen ideally in this world would come to pass, and even more. It is called the kingdom of God.

Is Eternal Life Forever?

A now-deceased member of my community of priests who was a beloved seminary teacher and choir director had a saying that was printed on his memorial card. He used to say: "Jesus offers you two promises. Your life has meaning, and you're going to live forever. If you get a better offer, take it." Naturally, it is hard to imagine a better offer. Jesus provides all we need. At the heart of his message is a promise of "eternal life" in God's kingdom (Matthew 25:46; Mark 10:30; John 3:15-16). But how should we view this in light of aging? Do we really want to live "forever"?

The concept of "eternal life" is only found in the New Testament. That is understandable, since Christianity developed the notion of life after death in the specific hope of everlasting life with God in God's kingdom. The seeds of this concept, however, are already found in later Old Testament literature, such as the Books of Maccabees or Wisdom, but the concept was fully formed only after the resurrection of Jesus. Indeed, his personal resurrection was totally unexpected, a surprise for his followers, even though he gave hints of it in his teaching (Matthew 17:23; Mark 10:34). In the Old Testament, the closest parallel is the concept of Sheol (Genesis 44:29; Psalms 9:17, 49:14), the shadowy underworld that awaits souls after death. It is not a true afterlife.

The very notion of a bodily resurrection brought great ridicule to Christian preachers. Remember the reaction of some in the Greek crowds on the Areopagus in Athens when Paul mentions the resurrection of Jesus as part of his message. "When they heard of the resurrection of the dead, some scoffed; but others said, 'We will hear you again about this'" (Acts 17:32).

The resurrection remains one of the most confusing aspects of Christian doctrine to many people today. One person has pestered me by email on a periodic basis demanding to know whether the New Testament envisions a physical, bodily resurrection or some other form. Some people commonly believe resurrection is only some sort of mental remembrance of our existence or living on "in spirit" in the thoughts and memories of loved ones. That is not the New Testament concept. The longest explanation of the resurrection in the New Testament is found in 1 Corinthians chapter 15. One key citation suffices to illustrate Paul's primary explanation.

> What I am saying, brothers and sisters, is this: flesh and blood cannot inherit the kingdom of God, nor does the perishable inherit the imperishable. Listen, I will tell you a mystery! We will not all die, but we will all be changed, in a moment, in the twinkling of an eye, at the last trumpet. For the trumpet will sound, and the dead will be raised imperishable, and we will be changed. For this perishable body must put on imperishability, and this mortal body must put on immortality. (verses 50-53)

Using imagery rooted in typical Jewish expectation of the end times (called "apocalyptic thought"), Paul explains at length that when the kingdom finally comes, God will indeed raise up our mortal bodies and transform them into spiritual bodies. The expression "will be changed" indicates something totally different, a full alteration of our existence. But even if it is a *transformation*, it is still a *physical* reality. It is not merely that we will be remembered for our deeds. Nor is it that we will live on in our descendants. It concerns the transformation—mysteriously, to be sure—of our natural, physical bodies into something supernatural and spiritual. Thus, from the perspective of faith, death is not the end, but a new stage in our existence. That is why the elderly are encouraged not to fear death, but to welcome it.

But do we really want *eternal* life? What does that mean? Some even wonder about growing older. If you knew for instance, that you were going to develop lung cancer and have a long period of suffering, difficulty breathing, and a slow death, would you voluntarily want that? Probably not. But if you knew in your old age that you would enjoy good health and a large measure of happiness, I assume most people would choose it. But the word "eternal" in the Bible can mean more than simply length of days. Yes, the mountains are "eternal" (Genesis 49:26; Habakkuk 3:6) in the sense that they seemingly last forever and do not change. (Geologically, we know this is not so; mountains grow, age, and diminish over time.) But when Jesus promises eternal life, it means also *quality* of life as well as unending length of days. In the Synoptic Gospels, Jesus ties eternal life in with proper fulfillment of the commandments (Matthew 19:16-20; Luke 10:25-28). But in those same passages, Jesus goes on to invite the hearer to do even more than merely observe the commandments. To truly inherit eternal life, one must become "perfect" by selling one's possessions and giving the proceeds to the poor (Matthew 19:21). Or one must reach out to one's "neighbor," understood as anyone in need, not simply those we like or live near (Luke 10:29-37, the parable of the Good Samaritan).

Hope for the kingdom of God is not just in the New Testament. It finds its roots also in the Old. In the Book of Isaiah, for instance, we find an interesting passage that speaks about how different things will be when God finally establishes his kingdom.

> For I am about to create new heavens / and a new earth; / the former things shall not be remembered / or come to mind. / But be glad and rejoice forever / in what I am creating; / for I am about to create Jerusalem as a joy, / and its people as a delight. / I will rejoice in Jerusalem, / and delight in my people; / no more shall the sound of weeping be heard in it, / or the cry of distress. / No more shall there be in it / an infant that lives but a few days, / or an old person who does not live out a lifetime; / for one who dies at a hundred years will be considered a youth, / and one who falls short of a hundred will be considered accursed. (65:17-20)

Here the image of reaching one hundred years of age is something totally extraordinary. It is only to be expected when God establishes a new kingdom. Reaching one hundred years of age is said to be the new benchmark. Anyone falling short of that will be "considered accursed." Ripe old age will be the norm; people will live out a full lifetime.

The Sunset of Life

One of the frequent images we encounter when speaking of the "golden years" is that they are meant to be like the sunset of life. Many people, perhaps most, appreciate a beautiful sunset. When I lived on the West Coast of the US in particular, I loved watching countless sunsets over the ocean. The colors that arrive as the sun seems to melt into the sea can be extraordinary. For me, these were always sacred moments. They were occasions to appreciate the gift of another day of life, and to anticipate yet another one on the horizon.

I suggest that the image of the sunset is a good one for reflecting on old age. After the sunrise and the noonday sun comes the sunset. Each moment has its precious components. Each second contains its unique gifts. And each stage of the day is meant to be savored.

We have been exploring what the Bible says about old age. I hope that this exploration has provoked some food for thought and also provided some comfort. If anything, the Bible teaches us that growing old is a gift from God.

It should be appreciated as the precious gift it is. God promises to accompany us on each step of the journey. Just when we think we do not have the energy to continue, God intervenes to lift us up. The Bible evokes an image for this endurance that comes from God: the eagle. This noble bird is a biblical image of endurance and strength. The psalmist uses it to recall God's care for us even as we age:

> Bless the LORD, O my soul, / and do not forget all his benefits / . . . who crowns you with steadfast love and mercy, / who satisfies you with good as long as you live / so that your youth is renewed like the eagle's. (Psalm 103:2, 4-5)

The God who lifted our distant ancestors up on eagle's wings (Exodus 19:4; Isaiah 40:31) promises to renew our strength as well. As we age, I hope we can maintain our confidence and our faith in this promise.

Many years ago, I read a book by John R. Powers, who expressed in fanciful fashion an image about growing old that has stuck with me.[12] In the book the main character, Conroy, writes letters to God seeking answers to life's mysteries. In one letter he asks, "Why do you let people grow old?" God's response comes back:

> Dear Conroy: Although I've created all of you, I often find the way you think quite puzzling. For me the most beautiful moment on earth is old people. They are my human sunsets. Signed: God.

For Reflection:

- How do you view the Christian teaching of the resurrection of the dead? Is it merely a pie in the sky? Is it a false promise? Do you have faith in what Jesus promised?

- How is it possible to live one's "golden years" when many times problems arrive that cloud the horizon? For you, how do you plan to grow old, should God allow you to do just that?

Afterword

We come to the end of our exploration of what the Bible says about old age. While the Bible does not address every modern problem associated with the increase of an aging population, we nevertheless find that the Bible does indeed offer some significant food for thought on the topic. Let me summarize some main ideas we have examined.

The first and most evident is that aging is part of the comprehensive process of human life. The norm of humanity is that people are born, they mature, they grow old, and they die. From a biblical perspective, God gives this life, and God takes it back. Job, whom we heard reflecting on the purpose of his life, declares: "Naked I came from my mother's womb, and naked shall I return there; the LORD gave, and the LORD has taken away; blessed be the name of the LORD" (Job 1:21). We are not our own masters. We are but creatures who share God's identity, male and female, but who do not share his eternal life in this world.

Second, under most circumstances, growing old is entirely normal. Not everyone gets a chance to taste it; some die young. If in biblical times, old age meant reaching forty, fifty, or sixty years of age—with rare instances of seventy or eighty—nowadays it often means surviving into one's eighties, nineties, and even beyond the century mark. The Bible nowhere claims that aging is easy. On the contrary, the Bible acknowledges the many challenges of growing old. But it is the norm for most human beings.

A third idea is that growing old is actually desirable. Old people help our collective human memory of what counts in this world, what values are most important. They also help retain the wisdom of the ages, making it possible to pass on to succeeding generations the sum and total of what counts in human existence. The elderly help us avoid missteps when we are young and impetuous. They also usually guide us along paths that are generally sure and straight.

A related and final thought is that aging is not to be feared. Old age is inevitably connected to impending death. It is natural for the elderly to ask what will become of them. Who will take care of them in their old age? Who will care for them when they are ill, incapacitated, bed-ridden, or handicapped? Who will attend to their remains when they die? These are natural fears. Yet old age itself is not be feared. It should be seen as the crown of one's life, the fulfillment of one's earthly journey as one prepares for the next step. People of faith believe that step to be eternal life with God and with the saints, our distant ancestors who await us. "Be not afraid" is a gospel refrain that older people should pray, like a mantra that reminds us that our life is not lived in vain. As we move to our personal golden sunset, let us boldly take some comfort in the reflections of the biblical authors we have explored in this little book.

Notes

1. See Jon L. Berquist, "The Biblical Age: Images of Aging and the Elderly," in *Graying Gracefully: Preaching to Older Adults* (ed. William J. Carl, Jr.; Louisville: Westminster John Knox, 1997), 48-51.

2. See Stephen Sapp, *Full of Years: Aging and the Elderly in the Bible and Today* (Nashville: Abingdon, 1987), 29. More recent statistics come from the National Center for Health Statistics, *National Vital Statistics Report*. 66:6 (Nov. 27, 2017).

3. Taken from https://en.wikipedia.org/wiki/Oldest_people (Accessed Feb. 9, 2019, 2:11 pm). Although one must very careful with data from Wikipedia, one can, with care, find useful and verifiable information there.

4. The passage is from Clement's work *Paedagogus* [Christ the Educator] and is quoted in Edwin M. Yamauchi and Marvin R. Wilson, *Dictionary of Daily Life in Biblical and Post-biblical Antiquity*, Vol. 1, A-Da (Peabody, MA: Hendrickson, 2014), 33.

5. The apocryphal book *Acts of Paul* (ca. 160 A.D.) and the Church Father John Chrysostom (d. 407 AD) assert this.

6. J.N.D. Kelly, *Jerome: His Life, Writings, and Controversies* (New York: Harper & Row, 1975), 295.

7. *Merriam-Webster's Collegiate Dictionary*, 11th ed. (Springfield, MA: Merriam-Webster, 2007), 432.

8. *Catechism of the Catholic Church*, 2nd ed. (Città del Vaticano: Libreria Editrice Vaticana, 1997), numbers 2276-2279.

9. *Catechism of the Catholic Church*, numbers 2280-2283, 2325.

10. Tweet, https://twitter.com/pontifex/status/1022443918389125120?lang=en, July 26, 2018, accessed April 8, 2019. See also Pope Francis's apostolic exhortation *Christus Vivit*, numbers 187-191.

11. Pontifical Council for the Laity. *The Dignity of Older People and Their Mission in the Church and in the World* (Washington, DC: USCCB, 1999), 41.

12. See John R. Powers, *The Unoriginal Sinner and the Ice-Cream God* (Chicago: Loyola Press, 2006; orig. 1977), 189.